Boulder, Colorado Births

1892–1906

An Annotated Index

Compiled by Dina C. Carson

Boulder, Colorado Births 1892–1906

An Annotated Index

Compiled by Dina C. Carson

Published by:
Iron Gate Publishing
P.O. Box 999
Niwot, CO 80544

All rights reserved. No part of this book may be reproduced or transmitted in any form or by any means, electronic or mechanical, including photocopying, recording or any information storage and retrieval system without written permission from the author, except for the inclusion of brief quotations in a review.

The Publisher of this directory makes no representation that it is absolutely accurate or complete. Errors and omissions, whether typographical, clerical or otherwise do sometimes occur and may occur anywhere within the body of this publication. The Publisher does not assume and hereby disclaims any liability to any party for loss or damage by errors or omissions in this publication, whether such errors or omissions result from negligence, accident or any other cause.

Iron Gate Publishing has used its best efforts in collecting and preparing material for inclusion in the *Boulder, Colorado Births 1892–1906: An Annotated Index*, but does not warrant that the information herein is complete or accurate, and does not assume, and hereby disclaims, any liability to any person for any loss or damage caused by errors or ommissions in the *Boulder, Colorado Births 1892–1906: An Annotated Index*, whether such errors or omissions result from negligence, accident or any other cause.

Copyright © 2012 by Dina C. Carson, Iron Gate Publishing

Printed in the United States of America

	ISBN	1-879579-79-0	ISBN 13	978-1-879579-79-8
eBook	ISBN	1-xxxxx	ISBN 13	xxxxxx

Introduction

This index has been compiled from the original birth records filled out by physicians after a birth and turned in to the County Clerk. The certificates were then recorded in the Birth Records Book, Volume 2, for Boulder County. Often the forms were not turned in until months after the birth. Based upon the form numbers recorded, there are many missing certificates for this time period.

There are many different types of forms in the records so the information available for each individual can be quite different. Many forms are incomplete. All of these forms were filled out by hand by the physician, and at times, the handwriting was challenging to read. Please consider phonetic or alternate spellings of names as you look through the list.

The more complete forms include the following information:

- the record number
- the child's name
- the child's color
- the child's sex
- whether the child was born alive or not
- the place where the child was born
- the hour and date
- the father's name and occupation
- the mother's maiden name
- where the parents lived at the time of the birth (often different than where the birth took place)
- the names of the other children (sometimes just the number of siblings)
- notes about any additional circumstances (including information about the death of the child or the death of one of the parents)
- the physician who attended the birth
- where the physician resided
- the date the form was filled out (or returned to the clerk) and
- the page and volume number where the birth was recorded

The original forms for Boulder Births, 1892-1906 are held by the Colorado State Archives and are accessible for research. You can order a copy of an original form from *Boulder Births, 1892-1906* by calling the Colorado State Archives or placing an order through their website.

Boulder, Colorado Births, 1892-1906

Abernathy,	1905 Nov 18 Abernathy, Martin L	W M Woods, Milie	
Abrams, Dora Ellen	1893 Sept 16 Abrams, Albert	W F Taylor, Sarah Annie	
Adair, Ada Belle Mary	1904 Sept 5 Adair, Andrew Adam	W F Barleau, Elizabeth	
Adams,	1893 Mar 12 Adams, Guy Arthur	W M Sharon, Annie	
Adams, Richard Thaddeus	1904 Oct 15 Adams, Jas B	W M Williams, Maude D	
Addams, Pearl	1893 Jan 1 Addams, J H	W F Brown, Lizzie	
Adler, Rachel	1893 Apr 7 Adler, Salomen	W F Berron, Minnie	
Agee, Kenneth	1898 July 8 Agee, Wm Grant	W M Murray, Izelle	
Akins,	1901 Dec 20 Akins, Chas	W M McGee, Sadie	
Allaback,	1904 July 7 Allaback, John Bud	W F Stansberry, Flora M	
Allaback, Wilbur	1902 July 18 Allaback, J B	W M Stansberry, Flora M	
Allcorn,	1902 Sept 21 Allcorn,	W M	
Allen,	1903 June 9 Allen, H W Jr	W M Richardson, Blanch	
Allen, Lillian	1898 Sept 20 Allen, O J	W F Brook, Alberta C	
Allen, Mildred	1897 Mar 23 Allen, Charles	W F Rhinesheimer, Marian	
Allison,	1897 Aug 19 Allison, Frank	W M Beale, Alta	
Anderson,	1902 May 21 Anderson, Fred	W M	
Anderson,	1904 Feb 4 Anderson, John August	W M Benson, Anna	

Boulder, Colorado Births, 1892-1906

Anderson,	1904 Oct 28 Anderson, Fred	W F ____, Bertha	
Anderson, Florence	1903 Sept 6 Anderson, Hilmer	W F Munson, Anna	
Anderson, Mildred Adeline Gertrude	1900 June 28 Anderson, John	W F Benson, Anna	
Andre,	1899 Nov 18 Andre, Albert	W F Parsons, Mattie	
Andrews,	1905 Sept 16 Andrews, John	W F Hall, ____	
Angove,	1892 Nov 17 Angove, Fred E	W M Neikirk, Fannie	
Appeldorn, Lou W	1902 May 1 Appeldorn, Walter	W M Bucheit, Emma	
Appledorn,	1904 Sept 29 Appledorn, Walter	W M Sidwell, Emma	
Applegren, Effie Delilah	1903 May 1 Applegren, Carl	W F Eskdahl, Alma	
Archibald, Robert Eldon	1903 May 15 Archibald, Chas H	W M Carrothers, Susie	
Ardourel, Helen A	1901 Nov 14 Ardourel, Theopholus	W F Friel, Amelia	
Aronowitch, Mildred	1895 June 28 Aronowitch, Louis	W F Bernhauer, Bessie	
Ashcroft,	1905 Apr 13 Ashcroft, C B	W M Stevenson, Ida	
Ashton, William H	1893 July 30 Ashton, David H	W M Titus, Effie M	
Atwood,	1901 Mar 8 Atwood, Joseph T	W F McCaslin, Adeline	
Austin,	1894 Dec 26 Austin, Eugene A	W F Phelps, Sarah S	
Autrey,	1898 June 6 Autrey, Thomas	W M Minks, May	
Autrey,	1904 June 6 Autrey, Roy Sterling	W F Birkett, Mary	

Boulder, Colorado Births, 1892-1906

Axelson,	1905 Mar 20 Axelson, G A	W M Mishle, Clare
Axelson,	1906 May 13 Axelson, G A	W M
Axford,	1905 Dec 14 Axford, Edwin	W F
Axford, Richard Samuel	1900 July 28 Axford, Ebenezer B	W M Berry, Harriet
Baber,	1905 Feb 10 Baber, Sam	W M Sauer, Maude
Bachelder,	1903 Sept 17 Bachelder, Wm A	W M Bachelder, Lula
Bailey,	1898 Jan 26 Bailey, Joseph R	W F Raybourne, Florence
Bailey,	1903 July 6 Bailey, Dwight B	W M Spicer, Etta
Bailey, Joseph R	1894 June 12 Bailey, Joseph R	W M Raybourne, Florence
Bair,	1905 July 30 Bair, Joseph H	W M Hill, Elizabeth
Baker,	1903 Aug 25 Baker, Peter	W F Costen, Edith E
Baker,	1904 Oct 2 Baker, Arthur	W M
Baker,	1906 Feb 14 Baker, John W	W M Smith, Susan A
Barbour, Mary Malvina	1905 June 11 Barbour, L P	W F Young, Mary
Barlow,	1903 May 29 Barlow, Chas T	W M Derr, Sarah
Barnett, Margurite Helen	1905 May 15 Barnett, Wm	W F Saggan, Minnie
Barry,	1901 Oct 13 Barry, Thomas E	W F Collins, Mary A
Bartlett,	1902 July 5 Bartlett, James	W M Wirick, Lulu

Boulder, Colorado Births, 1892-1906

Bartlett,	1892 Aug 20 Bartlett, Reuel	W F Holborn, Mary	
Bartlett,	1903 June 15 Bartlett, James	W F Wirick, Lulu	
Battey,	1894 Jan 14 Battey, Henry F	W M Cherry, Jessie F	
Battles,	1900 July 31 Battles, Geo W	W F Merrow, Leona	
Battles, Claude Otis	1902 Mar 12 Battles, L Bert	W M McIntyre, ____	
Baum,	1897 Sept 19 Baum, S W	W F Bottoms, Nannie J	
Baundy,	1906 May 31 Baundy, Wm	W F Smith, Mabel	
Baylor,	1894 Aug 28 Baylor, Chas N	W M Rowland, Lucy Ellen	
Bayse,	1906 June 10 Bayse, Guy	W F Mosher, ____	
Beals,	1905 Dec 6 Beals, John P	W F ____, Dora J	
Beard,	1897 June 16 Beard, Herman Mills	W F Machens, Ada P	
Beard,	1903 Apr 2 Beard, H W	W F Machens, Ada	
Beckstrom,	1902 Mar 7 Beckstrom, Frederick	W M Erickson, Lilly	
Beckwith, Frank Louis	1902 May 3 Beckwith, Leonard	W M Oest, Mary	
Begole, Lydia Marie	1900 July 24 Begole, Geo D	W F Stevenson, Mary	
Beidleman, Henry	1900 May 2 Beidleman, Oscar	W M Binns, Frankie	
Bellman,	1900 Jan 15 Bellman, W S	W F Kirkbride, Annie	
Bellman,	1902 July 18 Bellman, W S	W F Kirkbride, Anna	

Boulder, Colorado Births, 1892-1906

Bellman, Ruth	1898 June 17 Bellman, W S	W F	Kirkbride, Annie
Belser,	1895 Apr 1 Belser, Carl William	W F	Mischler, Susan
Bennett,	1903 May 3 Bennett, Clayton	W F	Johnson, Niti B
Benson,	1894 Aug 5 Benson, Thomas F	W F	Banglesdorf, GeorgeEtta
Benson,	1899 Mar 5 Benson, Pete	W M	Anderson, Anna
Benson,	1905 Mar 12 Benson, Nelse	W F	Blixt, Tholdo
Bergstrom,	1903 July 11 Bergstrom, Jno	W M	Johnson, Augusta
Berkley,	1895 Apr 26 Berkley, G M	W M	Slater, Jessie
Berkley, Benjamin	1898 Mar 15 Berkley, Frank	W M	Johnson, Minnie
Berkley, McKenzie	1899 Dec 12 Berkley, Frank	W M	Johnson, Minnie
Berkley, Roland	1895 Dec 24 Berkley, Frank	W M	Johnson, Minnie
Bernsten,	1895 Feb 27 Bernsten, Charles	W M	Andersen, Manda
Beyer,	1902 June 6 Beyer, George	W M	Teormu, Maggie
Billig,	1904 July 19 Billig, James A	W M	Catherwood, Grace Adele
Billig, William Clinton	1905 July 2 Billig, James A	W M	Catherwood, Grace Adele
Bixby, Wallace Edgar	1902 Mar 24 Bixby, Jesse A	W M	Wilson, Lena
Black, Ralph	1902 Aug 4 Black, David	W M	Gregg, Mabel

Boulder, Colorado Births, 1892-1906

Blackburn, Dorathen R	1897 Oct 20 Blackburn, Geo W	W	F Fry, Adalide M
Blackburn, Minerva	1905 Jan 28 Blackburn, Geo W	W	F Fry, Adelaide
Blosser, Ruby	1904 Feb 11 Blosser, Jacob	W	F Cantrall, Carrie
Blosser, Ruth	1904 Feb 11 Blosser, Jacob	W	F Cantrall, Carrie
Blum, Virginia	1901 June 25 Blum, Conrad	W	F Henry, May
Boche,	1906 June 9 Boche, Charles W	W	M Bonnel, Leonora
Bonelli,	1905 Sept 2 Bonelli, Paul	W	M
Booth,	1894 May 6 Booth, Walter Loyd	W	F Carr, Edna
Booth,	1901 Dec 17 Booth, Frank	W	M ____, Mamie
Booth,	1904 May 20 Booth, Frank	W	F Basanko, ____
Booth, Ezra Horace	1902 Mar 20 Booth, Walter L	W	M Carr, Edna
Borden,	1893 Feb 11 Borden, Edmund J	W	F Gilbert, Irene
Borden,	1901 Sept 17 Borden, E J	W	F Gilbert, Irene
Borden,	1903 July 14 Borden, E J	W	M Gilbert, Irene
Bottoms,	1893 Jan 29 Bottoms, Walter Lee	W	M Pickel, Lulu
Boulter, Phyllis	1892 Dec 29 Boulter, John	W	F Stewart, Mary
Boyd,	1898 Mar 28 Boyd, J W	W	F Martin, Julia
Bracy,	1896 Mar 26 Bracy, Daniel H	W	M Hunter, Sarah L

Boulder, Colorado Births, 1892-1906

Bracy, Ruby May	1898 Sept 14	W	F
	Bracy, Doul C	Hunter, Ella H	
Brand, Rudolph William	1903 Aug 14	W	M
	Brand, Frank B	Ayers, Alma	
Brandon,	1902 Nov 21	W	M
	Brandon, Jerry	Shapherd, Blanche	
Branford,	1903 Apr 13	B	M
	Branford, Alonzo	Willis, Anna	
Breach,	1892 Oct 27	W	F
	Breach, Fred	Markley, Sadie	
Brierly, Cecil	1895 May 26	W	M
	Brierly, Sylvester	White, Nanie	
Brister, Russell Laraine	1903 Oct 6	W	M
	Brister, Wm R	Randolph, Bertha	
Brockway, Alexander Grove	1899 May 4	W	M
	Brockway, W A	Grove, S S	
Brockway, Clara Mary	1893 Oct 6	W	F
	Brockway, William Ansley	Grove, Sarah Sophia	
Brohard,	1905 June 30	W	F
	Brohard, Thomas Marion	Cather, Alma May	
Bromley,	1893 May 1	W	F
	Bromley, Charles C	Mace, Myra M	
Bromley, Charles Dunham	1899 Nov 19	W	M
	Bromley, Charles C	Dunham, Theresa	
Bronson, Elmer	1902 Oct 8	W	M
	Bronson, Henry	Shear, Minnie	
Brooks,	1896 Apr 24	W	M
	Brooks, Frank	Urst, Mary	
Brooks,	1899 Oct 11	W	M
	Brooks, E P	Gill, ____	
Brooks,	1903 May 7	W	F
	Brooks, John W	Hussey, Maud M	
Brown,	1904 Nov 11	W	F
	Brown, A H	Chadbourne, Martha	
Brown,	1905 Mar 26	W	F
	Brown, Jno L	Thompson, ____	

Boulder, Colorado Births, 1892-1906

Brown,	1905 Dec 18	W F
	Brown, Chas C	Badgley, Margaret
Brown, Dorothy	1904 Jan 9	W F
	Brown, Jno L	Thompson, Carrie E
Brown, Margaret	1901 July 11	W F
	Brown, O N	Dutton, Flavilla
Brown, Newell Edward	1894 Oct 28	W M
	Brown, Charles Albert	Meeker, Edna
Brown,	1900 Dec 15	W M
	Brown, Charles A	Meeker, Edna
Brubaker,	1896 Apr 4	W F
	Brubaker, H	Larson, Emma
Bruddenbock, Marie	1899 July 21	W F
	Bruddenbock, William	Metz, Dena
Bryan, Ralph Arthur	1899 May 26	W M
	Bryan, Frank	Treadwell, Stella
Bryant,	1895 July 12	W F
	Bryant, J A	Maxwell, Alice A
Buckingham, Rosemary Greene	1905 May 29	W F
	Buckingham, Walter M	Greene, Janil B
Buffham,	1901 Aug 8	W M
	Buffham, Leslie	Euler, Isabelle
Bullard,	1905 Mar 13	W F
	Bullard, Otto W	
Burch,	1904 Apr 19	W F
	Burch, Willis E	Reedy, Martha A
Burger,	1902 Feb 17	W F
	Burger, Fred W	Faivre, Anna
Burger, Frances Marie	1900 Oct 2	W F
	Burger, Fred	Klinger, Clara
Burgess, Frankie	1902 July 16	W F
	Burgess, Bruce	Shaw, Mary
Buslen,	1896 Dec 6	W F
	Buslen, Miles R	Gordan, Cora L
Calden,	1899 Oct 22	W M
	Calden, Mike	Howell, Millie

Boulder, Colorado Births, 1892-1906

Calkins,	1896 Aug 10 Calkins, Alman	W M Gardner, Anna
Calkins,	1898 Apr 7 Calkins, Almon K	W M Orr, Anna Ellen
Calkins,	1901 July 15 Calkins, Almon K	W M Orr, Annie E R
Callahan, Katherine G	1904 Sept 23 Callahan, Gilbert A	W F Sawyer, Amy E
Callender,	1894 Nov 6 Callender, John L	W M Philpy, Olive G
Campbell,	1900 Dec 19 Campbell, Lee	W F Klee, Maggie T
Canall,	1894 July 22 Canall, Harry	W M Foreman, Elsie
Caper,	1903 [May] 29 Caper, Horace	W F Beary, Margaret
Carkener,	1897 June 24 Carkener, Geo S	W M Evans, Nell
Carlson,	1897 Oct 15 Carlson, John	W M Spurre, Hannah
Carmack,	1895 June 20 Carmack, John L	W M Mitchel, Siddie
Carpenter, Elihu	1904 Feb 23 Carpenter, W H	W M Monroe, Margerate
Carrie,	1894 June 6 Carrie, Alexander D	W M Titus, Luella B
Carsrud,	1905 Feb 11 Carsrud, Gus	W F Payne, Hattie
Casaday, Arthur Lockwood	1894 Apr 4 Casaday, Harry	W M Robertson, Elizabeth
Casey,	1901 Dec 31 Casey, Pat V	W F Towner, _____
Casey, Catherine Julia	1900 Nov 20 Casey, J H	W F Corning, Frieda
Casey, John H	1905 Feb 4 Casey, John H	W M Coring, Frieda

Boulder, Colorado Births, 1892-1906

Cattell, Bertha Luella	1906 Jan 16 Cattell, Wm P S	W F Wise, ____	
Cattermole,	1902 May 23 Cattermole, F P	W F Love, Cora M	
Cattermole, George	1900 Apr 6 Cattermole, G H	W M Stephenson, Marie	
Cattermole, Horace	1904 Jan Cattermole, F P	W M Love, Cora May	
Chamberlin [Chamberlain],	1900 Apr 11 Chamberlain, Pearl E	W F Lawrence, Cora	
Chandler,	1897 Feb 26 Chandler, Walt	W M Warner, Essie	
Chandler,	1898 Feb 11 Chandler, Walter	W M Warner, Essie M	
Chase, Harry Romeyn	1902 Jan 12 Chase, Romeyn	W M Jabas, Genevieve	
Chesney, Gwendolyn Virginia	1901 Apr 19 Chesney, Charles	W F Chase, Julia	
Childers,	1906 Nov 10 Childers, Thomas H	W F Ohelder, Hattie	
Ching, John Thomas	1903 Nov 13 Ching, Edward	W M Ching, Bertha	
Choate,	1893 Apr 1 Choate, Mortimer	W F Davis, Nellie	
Churchill,	1904 May 28 Churchill, Edmund	W M Sutton, Lillian	
Clark,	1892 June 3 Clark, Ellsworth A	W F Sailor, Alma	
Clark,	1897 Mar 9 Clark, E A	W M Sayler, Elinor	
Clark,	1898 Nov 2 Clark, E A	W F Sailor, Alma	
Clark,	1902 Sept 1 Clark, H M	W M Dalton, _____	
Clark,	1900 Feb 3 Clark, Roy R	W M Pease, Gertrude	

Boulder, Colorado Births, 1892-1906

Clark,	1903 Sept 14 Clark, Jesse E	W F Anthony, Mary R
Clark,	1904 Nov 15 Clark, J A	W M Davis, Gertrude
Cline,	1900 Sept 9 Cline, Robert W	W F Wilson, Ida
Cline,	1905 Apr 20 Cline, Robert W	W F Wilson, Ida
Coates, Edwin Wilder	1899 Nov 13 Coates, Edwin L	W M Wilder, Florence
Cobb,	1901 Feb 18 Cobb, Chas F	W F Thiel, Edith
Cobb,	1905 Sept 14 Cobb, Chas F	W M Thiel, Edith
Coffman,	1902 Dec 26 Coffman, Mitchell Hughes	W M Green, Maude
Colborn, Geraldine Hope	1903 Aug 19 Colborn, Jno A	W F McConnell, Nettie
Collins,	1905 June 22 Collins, W P	W F Eggleston, Louisa A
Collins, Angela	1901 Dec 27 Collins, William P	W F Eggleston, Louisa
Combs,	1903 Jan 20 Combs, Robt	W M Bradfield, _____
Coons,	1892 Sept 14 Coons, H R	W M Davis, Mina
Corbett, Pierce	1905 Oct 8 Corbett, Howard	W M Pierce, Lilly
Coslett, Ruth	1898 May 3 Coslett, James	W F Forbus, Ella
Coulehan,	1900 Sept 3 Coulehan, Charles E	W F Graves, Grace
Coulson,	1902 Aug 4 Coulson, Harry	W M Sheppard, Sadie
Craig,	1894 Mar 13 Craig, Clarence H	W M Harvey, Louise

Boulder, Colorado Births, 1892-1906

Craig,	1896 Nov 22 Craig, C H	W F Harvey, Louise	
Craig, Harry Becker	1903 Nov 13 Craig, Charles P	W M Becker, Clemence L	
Crary, John Howard	1893 Apr 11 Crary, J H	W M Boyer, Carrie	
Crawford,	1893 June 11 Crawford, Roy G M	W M Rodgers, Jennie F	
Crimmins,	1904 Apr 28 Crimmins, Bert	W M Schneider, Mollie	
Critchfield,	1899 Aug 11 Critchfield, Joe	W F Etteford, Ida	
Crockett, Katharine Thomas	1905 Feb 8 Crockett, Thomas W	W F Reed, Mary L	
Crosby,	1892 Apr 8 Crosby, Herbert	W M Anderson, Emma	
Crosby, Roscoe	1901 June 24 Crosby, Roscoe	W M Beeson, Isa	
Crosman,	1902 Aug 11 Crosman, Everett S	W M Richardson, Mary	
Crouch,	1892 May 24 Crouch, John E	W M Haitt, Ruphema	
Crouch, Frank	1902 Apr 28 Crouch, Stanton N	W M Winters, Katie	
Culbertson, Edward Alexander	1900 Mar 30 Culbertson, Charles	W M Hutchinson, Charlotte	
Curran,	1903 Oct 1 Curran, John	W M Warner, Minnie	
Curtis,	1905 Dec 5 Curtis, Geo C	W M Downs, Martha	
Curtis, Electa May	1893 May 9 Curtis, Frank Edward	W F Stanley, Ida	
Dalton,	1896 Aug 3 Dalton, Joseph	W F Spaulding, Lena	
Dalton,	1904 Jan 21 Dalton, Martin	W M Sherman, Anna	

Boulder, Colorado Births, 1892-1906

Dalton, Lenore	1906 May 26 Dalton, Isaac N	W F Sherman, Maude
Daugherty,	1902 Mar 20 Daugherty, Frank	W F Cummings, ____
Davis,	1892 Oct 24 Davis, Sidney C	W M Cole, Belle F
Davis, Kathleen Helen	1904 May 23 Davis, Abram A	W F Short, A Lyda
Dawson, Florence	1902 July 16 Dawson, Benj M	W M Hart, Bert
Day,	1903 Sept 20 Day, Timothy F M	W M Lachepelle, Ida
Day, Helen	1893 Apr 13 Day, John W	W F ____, Lizzie
DeBacker,	1898 June 23 DeBacker, Frank	W M Howard, Minora
Decker,	1894 Sept 22 Decker, Henry Snyder	W M ____, Izora
Demmon,	1904 Apr 19 Demmon, Wm R	W M Goddard, Edith E
Denham,	1892 Oct 4 Denham, Alonso	W M Smith, Jeanette
Denham,	1894 Feb 1 Denham, Alonso L	W M Smith, Jeanette Orr
Denham,	1903 Aug 25 Denham, A L	W M Smith, Janet [Jeanette]
DePriz,	1893 Feb 15 DePriz, Eugene	F Vogt, Christina
Derby,	1905 Sept 28 Derby, Fred	W M Wasley, ____
Derr,	1894 Mar 11 Derr, Joe E	W M Dalton, Susie
Derr, William	1895 Oct 8 Derr, Joe	W M Dalton, Susie
DeRusha,	1893 Mar 13 DeRusha, Elijah	W F McFarland, Mary

Boulder, Colorado Births, 1892-1906

Deutch,	1906 June 7 Deutch, P J	W	M
DeVoss,	1903 Feb 2 DeVoss, J Wm	W Sherer, Annie	F
DeWalt,	1904 Sept 14 DeWalt, Robert	W Trevarton, Edith	F
Dickensheets,	1906 Jan 1 Dickensheets, Larson	W Bradfield, Emma	F
Dickson,	1899 Oct 30 Dickson, Dennis H	W Youngblood, Marion J	F
Dittemore,	1899 Oct 22 Dittemore, James	W Eddy, Jessie	M
Dittemore,	1898 Sept 15 Dittemore, James H	W Eddy, Jessie A	F
Dittemore, Helen Alene	1901 Feb 24 Dittemore, James H	W Eddy, Jessie	F
Dole, Marion Emerson	1903 Aug 31 Dole, Harry E	W Franklin, Lulu	M
Donaghue,	1892 July 2 Donaghue, Terance	W Little, Maggie	M
Donaldson, John Andrew	1901 Apr 2 Donaldson, A R	W Parker, Mattie	M
Dragoo,	1901 Dec 27 Dragoo, Julius M	W Wolfesberger, Louisa	M
Dragoo,	1904 Nov 30 Dragoo,	W	M
Drumm, Alta Catherine	1900 Jan 6 Drumm, John B	W Morgan, Catherine L	F
Drummond,	1903 Aug 19 Drummond, Alvie	W Man, Bertha	F
Duane, William	1900 Oct 17 Duane, William	W Ravenal, Caroline Elsie	M
Dubi,	1893 Dec 25 Dubi, J J	W Ross, Florence	M
Duncan,	1895 May 25 Duncan, Robert A	W Wright, Myrtle May	M

Boulder, Colorado Births, 1892-1906

Duncan,	1895 Aug 20 Duncan, E E	W M Wright, Cena	
Duncan,	1898 Feb 4 Duncan, J M	W M Calton, Sue	
Duncan,	1899 Aug 15 Duncan, Robert A	W M Wright, Myrtle May	
Duncan,	1901 Sept 26 Duncan, John	W M	
Duncan,	1905 Jan 5 Duncan, John	W F Baldwin, May	
Duncan, Myrtle M	1901 Apr 29 Duncan, R A	W F Wright, Myrtle M	
Dungan,	1899 Sept 9 Dungan, F R	W M Randolph, _____	
Dunham, Edward Bennett	1896 Dec 2 Dunham, Maurice E	W M Bennett, A Janette	
Dunham, Helen Frances	1899 July 16 Dunham, Elbert L	W F Sambaugh, Ana M	
Dunn, Joe	1895 Mar 11 Dunn, Herbert	W M Harris, Claire M	
Durfee, Henry Gordon	1900 Oct 24 Durfee, Henry C	W M Corey, Etta	
Eastman,	1903 Aug 8 Eastman, Elmer O	W F Springsteel, Stella	
Eastman,	1905 Aug 18 Eatsman, Elmer	W F Springsteel, _____	
Eaton, Frank A	1894 Aug 1 Eaton, Robert	W M Flickenger, Maggie	
Edelhoff,	1899 June 26 Edelhoff, E	W M Anderson, Ana	
Ehrlich, Frieda	1898 Jan 30 Ehrlich, Louis	W F DeGroot, Ray	
Ehrlich, Marcella	1900 Apr 22 Ehrlich, Louis U	W F DeGroot, Rachel	
Elkins, Belra	1900 Aug 2 Elkins, Jesse R	B F Spieler, Melinda	

Boulder, Colorado Births, 1892-1906

Ellison,	1903 Aug 13 Ellison, A E	Light Brown F Scott, Annett
Epperly, Dewey	1899 Oct 15 Epperly, Howard	W M White, Susie H
Erickson, Arthur	1892 July 29 Erickson, Lewis	W M Eastland, Anna
Euler,	1894 Aug 31 Euler, Edward	W M Kelley, Hattie
Euler,	1898 Apr 2 Euler, R L	W M Lindley, Georgia L
Euler,	1903 June 15 Euler, Wm Jr	W M Cornell, Miss Clara
Euler, Emma	1892 Aug 20 Euler, Wm Jr	W F Cornell, Clara
Everitt,	1901 Mar 21 Everett, Delbert A	W M Edwards, Annie
Ewing, Howard Ellert	1897 Oct 19 Ewing, Frederick G	W M Springsteel, Dora
Fabrizio,	1905 Aug 10 Fabrizio, Peter A	W F Joratz, Frankie M
Faurot, L Alice	1894 Dec 10 Faurot, William Augustus	W F Terry, LaNicsa
Fields,	1902 Apr 24 Fields, Sanford	W M Liethe, Minnie
Figlia, Dominick	1905 Mar 13 Figlia, A	W M
Filion,	1906 June 24 Filion, Arthur	W M Cameron, Maud
Firstbrook,	1902 Sept 30 Firstbrook, Thomas	W F Struble, Grace
Firstbrook,	1903 Dec 5 Firstbrook, Thomas	W M Struble, Grace May
Fisher,	1895 Jan 21 Fisher, William Peter	W M Meeker, Estelle
Fisher, Julia	1897 Feb 3 Fisher, William P	W F Meeker, Estelle

Boulder, Colorado Births, 1892-1906

Foher, Lionel	1901 Aug 26 Foher, Lionel	W M	Lurman, Mary
Forsythe,	1895 May 26 Forsythe, Elijah E	W F	Mathews, Kate
Forsythe,	1902 Nov 24 Forsythe, E E	W F	Mathews, Kate
Fox,	1903 July 15 Fox, J Y	W M	Sachett, Carrie E
Fraser,	1905 May 13 Fraser, Geo W	W F	Sabin, Anna M
Frekes,	1897 July 17 Frekes, W H	W M	Gee, Mattie E
Friday,	1902 Sept 28 Friday, F J	W M	Anderson, Albertina
Friend,	1903 Oct 10 Friend, Chas	W M	____, Maud
Friend, Bernice Ethel	1902 Nov 15 Friend, Chas	W F	Atterberry, Jennie
Fry, William Clyde	1901 Mar 24 Fry, Chas	W M	Millin, Ivy Myrtle
Galattie,	1900 Apr 27 Galattie, Angus	W F	Raplon, Anna
Galusha,	1895 Jan 2 Galusha, Wm	W M	Shope, Rose
Galusha,	1903 July 4 Galusha, Benjamin F	W M	Rose, Gertrude
Gamble, Elizabeth Louise	1901 Feb 2 Gamble, Harry P	W F	Green, June Louise
Gardner,	1900 Dec 7 Gardner, F J	W F	Watts, Isabelle F
Gardner, Wm Hartley	1903 Sept 27 Gardner, Arthur C	W M	Richardson, Lilly
Gates, Clara	1892 July 18 Gates, Eugene E	W F	Palmer, Millie
Gause,	1906 Jan 19 Gause, Elmer O	W F	Main, _____

Boulder, Colorado Births, 1892-1906

George,	1895 Mar 24 George, W S	W	M Heivener, Doris
Gerhart,	1903 Sept 23 Gerhart, Charles	W	M Ericson, Lenni
Gerison,	1899 Nov 17 Gerison, George A	W	F Lundstrom, Hulda
Geromunger, Maud Etta	1899 May 5 Geromunger, William P	W	F Ferguson, Nettie
Giffin,	1893 Apr 24 Giffin, L M	W	F Lake, Fannie M
Giffin,	1894 Nov 13 Giffin, L M	W	F Lake, Fannie M
Giffin,	1898 Aug 27 Giffin, L M	W	M Lake, Fannie
Giffin,	1899 Nov 30 Giffin, Horace L	W	M McCammon, Annie
Giffin,	1901 Oct 18 Giffin, Horace L	W	M McCammon, Anna
Giffin, Grace Lake	1900 June 9 Giffin, L M	W	F Lake, Fannie M
Giggey, Clair Leon Morris	1894 Mar 7 Giggey, Charles	W	M Phillips, Belle
Giggy,	1903 Feb 19 Giggy, Leon	W	M Nelson, Mamie
Gilbert,	1899 May 27 Gilbert, Eduard	W	F _____, Nettie
Gilbert,	1901 Mar 11 Gilbert, Eduard	W	F Meyring, Nettie
Gilbert,	1906 Jan 4 Gilbert, Carson W	W	M Carroll, _____
Gilbert,	1906 June 15 Gilbert, Eduard	W	F Meyring, Nettie
Gilbert, Isabel Maurine	1903 Jan 31 Gilbert, Chas T	W	F Bumgarner, Daisy N
Gilbert, Mildred Jane	1903 Feb 11 Gilbert, Oscar M	W	F Kirkbride, Agnes

Boulder, Colorado Births, 1892-1906

Gilbert, Rachel	1905 Mar 12 Gilbert, O M	W F Kirkbride, Agnes
Gilbrand,	1898 Feb 15 Gilbrand, Charles T	W M Bumgarner, Daisy N
Gillard,	1896 Nov 30 Gillard, W W	W M Campbell, Lida
Giller, Charles Robert*	1897 Feb 15 Giller, Thos E *twins, one stillborn	W M Owens, Mary M
Giller, Janet	1902 Sept 28 Giller, Albert	W F Gilbert, Carrie
Gilmore,	1905 June 30 Gilmore, Jno T	W M Reardon, Mary
Girandet,	1901 Feb 14 Girandet, Frederick	W M Ceraton, Virla
Glazier,	1904 Mar 10 Glazier, Jas W	W F Wilcox, Ora
Goddard, Clint Morton	1904 Feb 6 Goddard, Frank M	W M Laughlin, Mable
Goddard,	1906 Apr 26 Goddard, Frank M	W M Laughlin, Mable
Goodro,	1904 Aug Goodro, Joseph	W M Myers, Martha
Goodwin,	1905 July 9 Goodwin, Walter	W M Urie, Jula
Gordeono,	1899 Sept 25 Gordeono, Glen	W M Musley, Annie
Gore, Eugene Herald	1898 Oct 10 Gore, R M	W M Edwards, Annie
Gothe, Mary Ellsworth	1898 Sept 1 Gothe, Victor E	W F Andrews, Susie May
Gould, Margaret Rachel	1900 Jan 12 Gould, Roy	W F Pomeroy, Leah
Graham,	1898 Sept 27 Graham, Chas J	W F Moses, Nora
Graham, Margaret	1906 May 10 Graham, Wm	W F

Boulder, Colorado Births, 1892-1906

Graham, Robert Elisha	1900 Aug 30　Graham, Robert E	W M	Luman, Bertha
Graves, Edgar Raymond	1902 Dec 9　Graves, John G	W M	Abbott, Alta
Green, Charles Arthur	1898 Jan 4　Green, William Henry	W M	Potter, Genevieve
Greene,	1905 Feb 6　Crandall, Don	W M	Greene, Cora
Gregg,	1894 July 3　Gregg, Frank	W M	Giggey, Lydia
Gregg,	1895 Feb 9　Gregg, Orlando W	W M	
Gregg, George Coabran	1892 July 23　Gregg, Orlando W	W M	Woods, Minnie
Gregg, Orlando G	1893 Oct 6　Gregg, Orlando W	W M	Pack, Minnie
Greisheim,	1906 Apr 15　Greisheim, R C	W M	Akins, Mary W
Greshaber,	1894 Spet 15　Greshaber, J C	W M	Foreman, Mabel
Greshaber,	1898 Mar 1　Greshaber, Joseph C	W F	Foreman, Mabel
Gross,	1904 Mar 2　Gross, Abner T	W F	Bohn, Clara F
Gross,	1905 Jan 30　Gross, C C	W M	Wedlake, Louisa Jane
Gross, George William	1903 Aug 30　Gross, C C	W M	Wedlake, Louisa
Gruier,	1906 Jan 30　Gruier, John G	W F	Abbott, Alta L
Gumeson,	1897 Oct 21　Gumeson, John	W M	Johnson, Amanda
Gunneson, Marguerite	1905 May 28　Gunneson, Chas	W F	Larsen, _____
Hagman, Charlotte Marie	1904 July 4　Hagman, Chas	W F	Hansen, Minnie

Boulder, Colorado Births, 1892-1906

Hagman, Melvin Andrew	1902 Dec 20 Hagman, Chas	W M
Hain,	1902 Oct 5 Hain, Wm	W M Johnson, Cora
Hales,	1904 June 12 Hales, C A	W F Muchenhaupt, Gail
Hall,	1899 May 7 Hall, G A	W M Forbes, Delia
Hall,	1903 Feb 18 Hall, Charles	W M Forbes, Delia
Hall, Dewey	1898 Sept 27 Hall, Welcome	W Dalton, Ella
Hall, Elizabeth M	1902 Oct 7 Hall, Welcome T	W F Dalton, Ella
Hall, William Earl	1902 Mar 9 Hall, Wm H	W M Newell, Mabel
Hallett, George	1897 Sept 21 Hallett, W H	W M Aumick, May
Ham,	1893 Sept 4 Ham, William H	W F Wolf, Harriet E
Hankens,	1904 July 14 Hankens, C E	W M Parks, Ida
Hankens, Ray Estef	1902 Sept 27 Hankens, C E	W M Parks, Ida L
Hanks,	1905 Sept 14 Hanks, William W	W M Cannon, Myrtle E
Hanson,	1897 Aug 4 Hanson, Andrew C	W M Nielson, Anna
Hardy,	1901 Dec 29 Hardy, Irving	W M Scofield, Mary
Harlow, Howatson	1903 Dec 12 Harlow, William Page	W M Howatson, Jean
Haroley,	1902 Oct 20 Haroley, LeRoy	W M Knaus, Tillie
Harris,	1906 Jan 3 Harris, William	W F Shumway, Maud E

Boulder, Colorado Births, 1892-1906

Harris, Walter Stewart	1903 Apr 10 Harris, Walter	W M	Binz [Binns], Bessie
Harrison, Benj F	1895 Aug 5 Harrison, Benj F	W M	Hollingsworth, Anna
Haslip,	1898 Nov 1 Haslip, William	W F	
Hatfield,	1904 Feb 6 Hatfield, Sidney A	W F	Stallings, Ora
Haugh,	1905 June 23 Haugh, Henry	W F	Jackson, Amanda
Haviland,	1900 Aug 23 Haviland, David A	W F	Wells, Leta
Haviland, Jean Delphine	1904 Feb 15 Haviland, David J	W F	Wells, Leta B
Hawkins, Elton E	1900 Nov 1 Hawkins, Elton E	W M	Foote, Adelaide
Hawkins, Ziemer	1903 Dec 26 Hawkins, Prince A	W M	Ziemer, Myrtle
Hayes,	1905 Jan 12 Hayes, W B	W M	Hipple, _____
Hays,	1899 Mar 17 Hays, Frank A	W F	Morton, Elsie R
Healy,	1905 Mar 5 Healy, Alva I	W M	Austin, Mathie
Hector, George	1902 Apr 24 Hector, Adolph A	W M	Gustafson, Charlotte
Hedeman, Frederika Matilda	1894 May 16 Hedeman, John F	W F	Larson, Matilda
Hedlund,	1905 Apr 2 Hedlund, Hayes	W M	Collinson, Selma
Hendon,	1899 July 10 Hendon, Erastus T	W M	Dollar, Mamie
Herkert,	1897 Sept 21 Herkert, Fred	W M	Reardon, Hannah
Herman,	1898 Jan 25 Herman, L (formerly Aronowitch)	W M	Bernhauer, Bessie

Boulder, Colorado Births, 1892-1906

Hetzel, Samuel D	1904 Jan 1 Hetzel, Sam J	W M Smith, C J
Hewitt,	1904 Aug 11 Hewitt, O E W	W F Tanner, Jane
Hickman, Helen Louise	1905 May 2 Hickman, Emmett	W F Wardenburg, Lulu
Hicks,	1903 July 10 Hicks, Joseph E	W M McAllister, Ethel
Hill,	1899 Mar 2 Hill, E T	W F Ory, Minnie
Hill,	1897 Nov 7 Hill, Edward L	W F Ary, Minnie M
Hill, George Barney	1893 June 27 Hill, Edward T	W M Ory, Winnie M
Hill, Matilda	1900 Apr 1 Hill, E B	W F Barton, Fannie
Hill, Ruth Blair	1898 Mar 27 Hill, Frank W	W F Primey, Ella
Hilton,	1902 Sept 17 Hilton, C W	W M
Hilts,	1892 Nov 19 Hilts, Samuel	W F Nelson, Harriet
Hinkle,	1897 Mar 18 Hinkle, J P	W M Quinn, Lillie
Hinman,	1895 Oct 26 Hinman, Curt	W F Shannon, Bertha
Hixson,	1903 Oct 23 Hixson, Howard	W F White, Vallie P
Hixson, Cathryn White	1902 Oct 1 Hixson, Howard	W F White, Vallie P
Hockaday,	1903 Dec 8 Hockaday, Edmund W	W F Haight, Grace
Hocking,	1899 July 2 Hocking, Wm W	W M Giggy, Myrtle
Hocking,	1902 Nov 15 Hocking, Elmer V	W F Eislinger, Lillie P

Boulder, Colorado Births, 1892-1906

Hocking,	1904 Aug 3 Hocking, E U	W M	Esslinger, Lillie
Hoffman,	1902 July 30 Hoffman, Cliff	W M	Fordis, Sarah
Holland,	1900 Apr 10 Holland, R O	W F	Newberry, Fannie
Holman,	1904 Jan 8 Holman, Thos B	W M	Anderson, Emma
Holstein, Beatrice Ruth	1900 Feb 4 Holstein, Harry C	W F	Levy, Rebecca
Hoover, William Rex	1905 June 18 Hoover, Wm L	W M	Fritter, Ruth
Hopper,	1903 Oct 22 Hopper, Thos P	W F	Hankins, Della
Horry, Grant Garfield	1893 Nov 11 Horry, James	W M	Frankfathers, Josephine E
Howe,	1905 Dec 26 Howe, Albert E	W F	McFadden, Lura D
Howell,	1892 Apr 8 Howell, Walker	W F	
Hoyer, Carl Walfred	1903 Nov 26 Hoyer, August L	W M	Anderson, Emma Christine
Hubbard,	1896 Apr 22 Hubbard, Charles	W M	Hudson, Maggie
Hubbard, William James	1894 Feb 17 Hubbard, William H	W M	Galusha, Mary
Hubbel,	1905 May 20 Hubbel, Theron E	W M	Wyatt, _____
Hubman, Karl	1905 Feb 7 Hubman, Chas	W M	Price, Ellen
Hugeltno, Alice Lucretia	1905 Mar 8 Hugeltno, John	W F	Carr, Lois
Hull,	1897 Aug 10 Hull, Grant	W F	Snyder, Katie
Hunt, Linfield Harold	1902 June 15 Hunt, Linfield V	W M	Sykes, Georgiana E

Boulder, Colorado Births, 1892-1906

Hupp, (twin)	1905 Oct 16 Hupp, Wm	W M	Heck, Myral
Hupp, (twin)	1905 Oct 16 Hupp, Wm	W F	Heck, Myral
Huschleffe,	1905 Apr 30 Huschleffe, J N	W M	Freman, Elsie
Imel,	1896 Dec 8 Imel, Alonzo C C	W F	Jay, Rosa
Infield, *	1905 May 14 Infield, J H	W F	Boline, Catherine

*twin girls, one died soon after birth

Ingalls, Harvey Munson	1905 May 3 Ingalls, Harry D	W M	Haskey, Georgia
Ingals,	1905 June 26 Ingals, M	W F	Kinsman, _____
Ingram, Edwin	1905 Jan 6 Ingram, E J	W M	Faivre, Louise
Isard, Frances	1902 July 8 Isard, Alva	W F	Snook, Nellie
Jacka,	1892 Apr 27 Jacka, Thos	W M	McIntosh, Jennie
Jacka, Marion M	1894 Sept 10 Jacka, Thos	W F	____, Jennie B
Jackson,	1896 July 15 Jackson, F H	W M	Fuller, Grace
Jacobson,	1903 May 16 Jacobson, Nils	W M	Boystatt, Marie
Jain,	1897 Apr 19 Jain, Ben	W M	Wellman, Belle
Jain,	1903 Jan 9 Jain, B F	W M	Wellman, Clara B
Jain,	1904 Sept 7 Jain, B F	W M	Wellman, Belle
Jain, Zerleta	1902 May 26 Jain, Clyde	W F	Borlan, Hattie
James,	1894 Oct 18 James, Alex	B M	Block, Jennie

Boulder, Colorado Births, 1892-1906

James,	1904 May 31 James, Alfred	W F Jones, ____
Jenner, Delbert Oren	1902 Oct 5 Jenner, William	W M Sweet, Nellie
Jermo, Beatrice	1902 Nov 1 Jermo, Andrew	W F Bailey, Maggie E
Johnson,	1893 Mar 12 Johnson, Frank	W F Ninsie, Artie
Johnson,	1898 July 28 Johnson, Amos	W M Anderson, Mary
Johnson,	1903 Oct 1 Johnson, Peter C	W M Larson, Emma
Johnson,	1904 Mar 18 Johnson, Wm A	W M Allen, Daisy M
Johnson, Alvah	1898 Apr 6 Johnson, Wesley	W M Brown, Sara
Johnston,	1893 May 27 Johnston, Wm J	W M Adams, Clare
Johnston,	1899 Aug 11 Johnston, William J	W F Adams, Clara
Johnston, Lawrence Allen	1902 Dec 8 Johnston, Frank	W M Montgomery, Hattie
Johnston, Louis R	1893 Jan 8 Johnston, Louis R	W M Walker, Helen Jane
Jones,	1895 Oct 4 Jones, Mark	W F Heller, Della
Jones,	1899 May 10 Jones, Frank	W F Hill, Alya
Jones,	1904 Nov 7 Jones, Earl R	W F Holly, Josie
Jones, Dorr Theophilus	1893 Sept 12 Jones, Daniel Thomas	W M Low, Clara Ellen
Joratz,	1905 May 9 Joratz, Joe	W F Chasino, Mary
Jordinelli, Frank	1900 Jan 18 Jordinelli, John	W M Dovina, Rose

Boulder, Colorado Births, 1892-1906

Joss, Wm	1902 Sept 20 Joss, Wm	W M	Cheyne, Annie
Joss, Wm	1905 Apr 21 Joss, Willie	W M	Cheyne, Annie
Joyce, William Edward	1892 Nov 20 Joyce, Bernard	W M	House, Melissa Jane
Junior,	1893 Jan 22 Junior, Adolph	W M	Woods, Minnie
Kaler, Charles F	1905 Mar 23 Kaler, Fred H	W M	Smith, Nevada
Karns,	1904 Jan 16 Karns, John P	W F	Harris, Margarett
Kealiher,	1903 Mar 2 Kealiher, Clarence	W F	Bond, Bertha
Kellogg,	1900 July 14 Kellogg, M M	W F	Wood, Ruth
Kemmler,	1904 Jan 28 Kemmler, Ernest	W F	Etz, Emma
Kendrick,	1906 July 2 Kendrick, Sam	W M	Storey, Ida
Kerr,	1898 Apr 26 Kerr, C E	W F	Mathews, Lida
Kestle, Preston	1898 Mar 24 Kestle, Thomas	W M	Phillips, Anna
Killier, Thurllyn	1900 Feb 26 Killier, David	W M	Craig, Jennie
King,	1894 May 4 King, Wm F	W M	Sida, Mary
King,	1905 July 11 King, J N	W F	Hardin, Clara S
Kingman, Annie	1894 Sept 7 Kingman, Henry	W F	Lee, Annie
Kinsman,	1904 Nov 28 Kinsman, F J	W F	Taylor, ____
Kittle, Josephine Blanche	1900 Nov 10 Kittle, Harl S	W F	Cork, Josephine

Boulder, Colorado Births, 1892-1906

Knapp,	1904 Dec 4 Knapp, Geo	W	F
Knight,	1899 July 9 Knight, Harry	W Kern, Estella	M
Knight,	1906 May 17 Knight, Harry	W	F
Knight, George	1894 Jan 8 Knight, Harry Stewart	W Keen, Estella L	M
Knopf,	1893 Feb 25 Knopf, E J	W Robinson, Annie S	M
Knott,	1892 Oct 31 Knott, Sam'l G	W Mitchel, Lizzie	F
Knowlton, George Theodore	1901 Nov 6 Knowlton, Carroll F	W Stephens, Elsie	M
Knox, Randolph B	1905 Apr 2 Knox, Chester	W Bradway, Ruth	M
Kohler,	1899 May 28 Kohler, Fred Jr	W McCall, Francis	M
Kohler,	1902 May 26 Kohler, Fred Jr	W McCall, ____	F
Kohler,	1902 Nov 6 Kohler, Charles S	W Carner, Rose	M
Kramer, Frederick Sprague	1892 Sept 10 Kramer, Frederick Ferdinand	W Sprague, Ada Josephine	M
Kramer, John Spalding	1893 Nov 17 Kramer, Frederick Ferdinand	W Sprague, Ada Josephine	M
Kuhepass,	1905 May 11 Kuhepass, Geo A	W Sorley, Anna	F
Labbo,	1900 Mar 4 Labbo, Frank	W Rappa, Maggie	F
Lacer,	1904 Aug 14 Lacer, Chas	W Vernon, Essie	M
Lake,	1902 July 27 Lake, H C	W Butler, Olive	F

Boulder, Colorado Births, 1892-1906

Lake, Mary Marguerite	1900 Apr 24 Lake, H C	W F Bueler, Olive
Lakin,	1897 Nov 27 Lakin, Frank	W M Raikes, Grace W
Lamb, Ogden Frances	1903 June 28 Lamb, M T	W M Ogden, Anna
Lambert,	1902 Aug 16 Lambert, Fred	W F Jump, _____
Lamm, Alice	1895 Dec 16 Lamm, Wm	W F Sheppard, Ida
Larsen,	1895 Dec 12 Larsen, C R	W M Peters, Pauline
Larson,	1895 Mar 21 Larson, William John	W M Williams, Mabel
Larson,	1904 Jan 26 Larson, Albert	W F Johnson, Bettie
Larson,	1905 Dec 6 Larson, Albert	W M Anderson, Nora
Larson, Mildred	1899 Aug 9 Larson, Peter A	W F Wallace, Mae
Latora,	1892 Aug 24 Latora, Felix	W M
Laurence,	1899 July 20 Laurence, Albert	W M Chambers, Mary
Law,	1901 Aug 12 Law, Howard	W F Urich, Daisy
Lawrence,	1903 Mar 7 Lawrence, Henry	W M Sellers, Mattie M
Lawrence,	1904 June 12 Lawrence, D E	W F Hinkle, _____
Lawson,	1897 Feb 24 Lawson, William S	W F Smith, Ada
Lee,	1897 May 13 Lee, John H	W M Higgins, Mary
Leech, Dorothy	1892 May 22 Leech, William F	W F Goslen, Emma

Boulder, Colorado Births, 1892-1906

Leland,	1905 July 6 Leland, Lyman W	W M Allen, Jennie
Lemmex, Iola Elizabeth	1901 May 14 Lemmex, Frank	W F Harris, Della
Lennertz,	1903 May 20 Lennertz, Herman	W F Hecker, Elizabeth
Levinton, (twins)	1898 Nov 20 Levinton, James	W F Bush, Maud
Lewis,	1895 Mar 25 Lewis, W C	W F Giggey, Laura
Lewis,	1897 Feb 12 Lewis, Grant	W M Engert, Daisy
Lewis,	1897 Oct 8 Lewis, Edward	W M Rockwell, Mamie
Lewis,	1905 Mar 8 Lewis, Harry	W M Jester, Loretta
Lewis,	1905 Mar 30 Lewis, O A	W M Evans, Sadie
Lewis, E C Jr	1897 Feb 24 Lewis, E C	W M Milligan, Fannie O
Lewis, Helen	1905 Mar 8 Lewis, Harry	W F Jester, Loretta
Lewis, Kenneth Carr	1894 July 8 Lewis, Nathaniel	W M Carr, Edith
Lewis, Nathaniel Fancy	1897 Mar 28 Lewis, Nat	W M Carr, Edith
Libby, Eleanor Clare	1902 May 1 Libby, M F	W F Phillips, Agnes
Lilly,	1893 Apr 21 Lilly, John E	W M Barnes, Evaline L
Lincoln,	1892 Dec 22 Lincoln, Stanton	W F Wright, Nellie
Linder,	1906 Jan 25 Linder, Chris	W M Eggler, ____
Lindermann, Ernest	1905 Oct 21 Lindermann, Reece	W M Whyte, Ruth Margaret

Boulder, Colorado Births, 1892-1906

Lindstrom,	1899 Dec 5 Lindstrom, Chas	W	M
Lines	1897 May 19 Lines, G W	W Edwards, Bertie	F
Lines,	1900 Dec 5 Lines, G W	W Edwards, Bertie	M
Lingham, Abraham	1906 Feb 12 Lingham, Frank	B Scruggs, Lulu	M
Litch, Rodney Marion	1905 June 11 Litch, H F	W Rockwood, Emma	M
Loach, William Jennings	1905 Apr 9 Loach, William	W Todd, Violet H	M
Long,	1898 Sept 13 Long, Leon	W Holt, Ora	F
Long,	1901 Sept 11 Long, Charles W	W Bruet, Luvella M	F
Longhi,	1894 Nov 18 Longhi, Albert W	W Rider, Cora	M
Loofboro,	1897 June 25 Loofboro, Chase A	W Forsythe, Tamer	
Louth,	1900 Mar 18 Louth, James	W	F
Lowe,	1902 June 7 Lowe, J M	W	M
Lowrey, Mary	1893 May 23 Lowrey, Charles Emmet	W Thompson, Mary Glover	F
Lunburg,	1901 May 1 Lunburg, Gustove E	W Emanual, Alma	F
Lundrie,	1897 July 7 Lundrie, Peter P	W Johnson, Jennie	M
Lurvid,	1902 Feb 25 Lurvid, Charles	W White, Emma	M
Lynor, Elizabeth	1900 Apr 7 Lynor, John M	W Cronin, Elizabeth	F
Lyon,	1903 Jan 9 Lyon, Edgar	W Eubank, Maude	M

Boulder, Colorado Births, 1892-1906

Mackey,	1893 Feb 9th Mackey, Richard	W M	Slattery, Mary
Magee, Catherine	1902 Nov 12 Magee, John	W F	Dalton, Julia
Marian,	1896 Apr 1 Marian, John	W M	Vance, Mary
Marino,	1905 June 29 Marino, Joseph	W M	Fondi, Josephine
Marr,	1904 Dec 26 Marr, Wm Nolan	W F	Kenyon, Della
Marriott,	1904 May 22 Marriott, Fred	W M	Carlton, Jane
Marro,	1905 Mar 27 Marro Antonio	W M	
Marshall, Neata Agnes	1899 July 27 Marshall, R T	W F	Fink, Emma
Martin,	1893 Oct 16 Martin, Wm R	W M	Thayer, Myrtle
Martin, John	1894 Mar 26 Martin, Samuel	W M	Blair, Mary
Mason,	1899 Apr 28 Mason, J D	W F	Mila, Josie
Mason,	1904 Sept 4 Mason, Geo W	W M	Pinkham, Abigail
Mason, Barbara	1901 Feb 5 Mason, E C	W F	Richards, Jennie
Mason, Isabel	1901 Feb 5 Mason, E C	W F	Richards, Jennie
Mathews,	1896 Dec 29 Mathews, Frank	W M	Beole, Nora
Matters,	1893 Feb 18 Matters, Thos	W F	Littlejohn, Elizabeth
Maxwell, Della	1893 Jan 24 Maxwell, Charles Alonzo	W F	Davis, Mary
Mayad, Ada Louise	1896 Aug 27 Mayad, Harry	W F	Tulley, May

Boulder, Colorado Births, 1892-1906

Mayad, Samuel Tully	1895 Feb __ Mayad, Harry	W M Tulley, May
Mayall, Henry Hale	1900 Nov 30 Mayall, Harry	W M Tully, May
Mayall, May Lucy	1902 Oct 13 Mayall, Harry	W F Tully, May
Mayall, Sarah J	1905 Apr 17 Mayall, Harry	W F Tully, May
McAllester, Marion E	1902 Feb 27 McAllester, Daniel E	W F Hankins, Lula
McAllish, Marjorie Mansfield	1900 Dec 5 McAllish, Daniel Eldridge	W F Hankins, Lula
McCall,	1892 Nov 15 McCall, George	W F Downs, Rose
McCall, George Willard	1894 June 29 McCall, George	W M Downs, Rose
McCare,	1899 Dec 13 McCare, John	W F White, Ella
McCarl,	1905 Mar 20 McCarl, Elsworth	W F Campbell, Birtha
McClora,	1894 June 18 McClora, A	W M Hull, Ella
McClure,	1905 Dec 4 McClure, George A	W M Evan, Edith
McColly,	1903 Dec 22 McColly, James F	W M Hoke, Mary
McConnell,	1905 Feb 2 McConnell, Porter	W F Miller, ____
McDonald, Sarah Isabelle	1905 Jan 20 McDonald, Jas	W F McLean, Christine
McDowell,	1893 July 31 McDowell, Andrew S	W M Davis, Mary M
McFadden,	1904 Nov 17 McFadden, Lou S	W M Miles, Lizzie
McGinnis,	1902 Apr 24 McGinnis, Wm	W M Bottoms, Catherine

Boulder, Colorado Births, 1892-1906

McKelvey,	1905 Nov 25	W	F
	McKelvey, Roy E	Cowan, Elsie F	
McKenna,	1900 jan 28	W	M
	McKenna, Harry	Kellogg, Nellie	
McLilton,	1903 Nov 17	W	M
	McLilton, Eugene E	Howard, Cora	
McLinnis,	1898 Sept 29	W	M
	McLinnis, John	Halps, Georgiana C	
McLinnis,	1900 July 24	W	M
	McLinnis, John	Helps, Georgina	
McMasters, Barbara	1903 Feb 15	W	F
	McMasters, P H	Short, Sarah	
McMillan,	1901 Feb 3	W	M
	McMillan, F H	Crosby, Jennie	
McVey,	1895 Nov 14	B	F
	McVey, J	Bailey, Emma	
McVey,	1899 June 5	B	F
	McVey, J D	Bailey, Emma	
McVey,	1900 Sept 4	B	F
	McVey, J D	Bailey, Emma	
McVey,	1904 Feb 1	B	M
	McVey, J W	Bailey, Emma	
Mecham, Paul Willis	1905 Jan 28	W	M
	Mecham, Edward U	Beall, Elsie	
Meginnes, Harold	1898 Sept 16	W	M
	Meginnes, W H	Balderson, Katherine	
Meikle, Agnes	1906 Jan 16	W	F
	Meikle, Geo	Fagerstedt, _____	
Meikle, Archibald	1900 Sept 15	W	M
	Meikle, Archibald	Williams, Maggie	
Mellor, Margaret Elizabeth	1895 Aug 10	W	F
	Mellor, James Herbert	Wade, Arminta	
Mendenhall,	1900 July 12	W	M
	Mendenhall, Elisha F	Harris, Emma	
Meredith, Leland	1902 Oct 19	W	M
	Meredith, J Q	Stevens, Belle	

Boulder, Colorado Births, 1892-1906

Merrill, Myrtle Zoella	1892 Nov 23	W	F
	Merrill, E T	Miller, Hattie	
Messenger, Elmer	1901 Dec 25	W	M
	Messenger, Claudius L	Yerkey, Carrie	
Metcalf,	1892 May 12	W	F
	Metcalf, Lewis M	Clark, Mattie	
Metcalf,	1894 June 17	W	F
	Metcalf, L M		
Metcalf,	1901 Oct 19	W	F
	Metcalf, Frank P	White, Minnie Ada	
Metcalf, Laura Lee	1896 June 9	W	F
	Metcalf, Geo E	Meisele, Johanna	
Meyer,	1901 Oct 16	W	M
	Meyer, Max	Rachofsky, Dora	
Michelson,	1898 Feb 9	W	M
	Michelson, John W	Grusbury, Cora	
Middleton,	1902 July 16	W	F
	Middleton, W W	Moore, Mary L	
Middleton,	1903 Aug 4	W	M
	Middleton, Wm W	Moore, Mary L	
Middleton, Theron Cecil	1904 Dec 5	W	F
	Middleton, W W	Moore, Mary L	
Miles,	1904 Feb 18	W	M
	Miles, Leslie P	Garborino, Lida	
Milker,	1902 Nov 6	W	F
	Milker, H H	Reid, Nellie	
Miller,	1898 Aug 25	W	M
	Miller, J O	Whitsell, Maud	
Miller,	1899 Oct 18	W	M
	Miller, Arnold	Morrison, _____	
Miller,	1902 Nov 9	W	F
	Miller, G E	Ross, Eunty	
Miller, LeRoy H	1902 Mar 5	W	M
	Miller, John O	Whitsett, S Maud	
Milne,	1898 Apr 27	W	M
	Milne, Robert	Noel, Ethel	

39

Boulder, Colorado Births, 1892-1906

Milner,	1902 Nov 3	W	M
	Milner, Harvey E	Hite, Cedella	
Mitchel,	1896 May 10	W	M
	Mitchel, Fred	Shute, Pearl A	
Mitchell,	1905 Nov 5	W	M
	Mitchell, Chase	Sly, Bessie	
Mitchell, John Charles	1897 June 11	W	
	Mitchell, Fred	Shute, Pearl A	
Mock,	1898 Nov 2	W	F
	Mock, Will T	Davidson, Adeline	
Mock,	1902 Sept 1	W	M
	Mock, Isaac	Farley, Mabel	
Moeller,	1906 July 22	W	F
	Moeller, Peter	Hurtencin, Alma	
Money,	1902 Aug 20	W	M
	Money, Kenneth	Thompson, Carrie E	
Monroe,	1901 June 25	W	M
	Monroe, D N	Anderson, Gussie	
Monroe, D N	1899 Dec 16	W	M
	Monroe, D N		
Montgomery,	1903 May 12	W	M
	Montgomery, Walter A	Burlingame, Edna M	
Montgomery, Jack Reemier	1903 July 7	W	M
	Montgomery, B L	Townsend, Margaret	
Moon,	1902 Sept 7	W	M
	Moon, John D	Williams, Emma A	
Moon, Anna Lucylle	1903 Nov 23	W	F
	Moon, Williw O	Hillberry, Ella M	
Moore, Catherine Gertrude	1896 Feb 4	W	F
	Moore, William Y	McGady, Catherine	
Morrell, Irene Frances	1902 Oct 24	W	F
	Morrell, Anthony	Ludlow, Julia	
Morrison,	1902 Oct 16	W	M
	Morrison, M S	Montgomery, Nellie	
Morro,	1903 May 2	W	M
	Morro, Antonio		

Boulder, Colorado Births, 1892-1906

Moseley, Geo B	1896 Apr 10 Moseley, C B	B M	Wade, Arm
Mosely, Luekan Garber	1900 Feb 11 Mosely, Chas B	B M	Lorpee, Georgia
Mudd,	1903 Aug 4 Mudd, Don Alexis	W F	Davis, Mary E
Mudd,	1905 May 12 Mudd, Don A	W M	Davis, Emma
Munson, William LeRoy	1902 Aug 5 Munson, A L	W M	Davis, Agnes
Murphy,	1905 Jan 8 Murphy, G H	W M	Cacheman, Margaret
Mushblond,	1897 May 21 Mushblond, Edgar	W M	Kempton, Mabel
Myers,	1905 Mar 7 Myers, Jas M	W M	White, Daisy
Neiheisel, Dorothy Grace	1905 Oct 31 Neiheisel, Wm	W F	Aumick, ____
Nelmer,	1899 Dec 31 Nelmer, Charles	W F	Tyler, Bessie L
Nelms,	1903 Nov 14 Nelms, Hubert	W F	Mathews, ____
Nelson,	1893 Apr 25 Nelson, James	W M	Brown, Leona
Nelson,	1897 June 11 Nelson, Alexander	W M	Selcott, Alice
Nelson,	1900 July 17 Nelson, Petrus	W M	Lauretzen, Katy
Nelson,	1903 Mar 9 Nelson, Arvi	W M	Gumeson, ____
Nelson, Anna	1900 Jan 21 Nelson, P B	W F	Petersen, Inya M
Nelson, Ernest	1902 July 17 Nelson, N P	W M	Nelson, Selma
Nelson, Ethel	1904 Sept 28 Nelson, L R	W F	Baldwin, Inez B

Boulder, Colorado Births, 1892-1906

Nelson, Lois Marie	1898 May 10 Nelson, Adam W	W F Hendter, Elizabeth
Neufert,	1902 Apr 24 Neufert, Chadwick	W F Tracy, Adelina
Neville,	1905 June 18 Neville, Chesley W	W M Oden, ____
Newcomb, Laura Leola	1899 July 30 Newcomb, Clarence W	W F Kelly, Gerdie L
Newhouse,	1897 May 29 Newhouse, Harry R	W M Veslick, Hattie
Nichols,	1902 Oct 13 Nichols, Walter H	W F Connor, Esther
Nichols,	1906 Feb 26 Nichols, Webb W	W M ____, Minnie F
Nicholson,	1892 July 7 Nicholson, J H	W F Hoyle, Camie
Niederber,	1896 Nov 16 Niederber, Frank	W M Boecker, Mary L
Nordquist,	1903 Nov 6 Nordquist, Nels	W F Larson, Jennie
Norlin, Agnes Margurette	1905 Apr 15 Norlin, George	W F Dutcher, Minnie
Norman,	1892 July 17 Norman, R C	W M Flannery, Lena
Norman,	1894 June 22 Norman, R C	W F
O'Connor, Daniel	1902 Nov 29 O'Connor, Clarence J	W M Clark, Elvira Virginia
O'Connor, Jno Robert	1903 July 7 O'Connor, Jno	W M Hall, Harriett
O'Connor, Robert Clark	1901 Jan 5 O'Connor, Clarence J	W M Clark, Elvira Virginia
Ogden,	1905 Mar 18 Ogden, Eugene	W F Tydeman, Carrie
Oliver,	1896 Aug 17 Oliver, Will J	W M Bromley, Alice

Boulder, Colorado Births, 1892-1906

Oliver,	1900 July 5	W	M
	Oliver, John N	Bromley, Alice	
Osborn,	1901 Dec 12	W	F
	Osborn, Chas	Firth, _____	
Otis,	1898 July 30	W	M
	Otis, Hampton J	Randolph, Geraldine	
Owen, Lucrete B	1900 Sept 16	W	F
	Owen, William C	Peterson, Minnie	
Paddock, Kenneth Larden	1897 Sept 1	W	M
	Paddock, Frank Smith	Mansen, N Campbell	
Page, Harry J	1899 Dec 11	W	M
	Page, Frank K	Retallack, Louise	
Page, Ralph Attebury	1901 Feb 23	W	M
	Page, Andrew F	Attebury, Ella	
Palmer,	1906 Jan 3	W	M
	Palmer, Henry H	Strottemire, Lula May	
Palmer, Dorothy Hamilton	1893 Aug 11	W	F
	Palmer, Frederic Armine	Hamilton, Clara Louise	
Palmer, Winifred W	1896 May 18	W	F
	Palmer, Chas P	Warner, Harriet	
Parcells, Arthur	1898 July 9	W	M
	Parcells, E W	Spicer, Julia	
Parks, Alvin Thomas	187 Aug 29	W	M
	Parks, Geo B	Maxwell, Ada	
Parks, Reuel Lois	1892 Nov 24	W	F
	Parks, Geo B	Maxwell, Ada	
Parsons,	1901 Oct 12	W	M
	Parsons, J A	Blomquist, Emelia	
Parsons, Margaret Eliza	1905 Apr 8	W	F
	Parsons, Joseph H	Phillips, Emily	
Parsons, William James	1899 Apr 8	W	M
	Parsons, Joseph	Philips, Emily	
Pate, Ethel Pearl	1902 July 26	W	F
	Pate, Edgar	Smith, Bertie	
Patterson,	1893 Jan 16	W	M
	Patterson, Orlando	Baker, Emma	

Boulder, Colorado Births, 1892-1906

Patterson,	1901 Dec 17 Patterson, Orlando	W M Baker, Emma	
Patton, Mada	1901 Oct 14 Patton, A C	W F	
Peasley, LeRoy Verner	1902 Oct 29 Peasley, LeRoy	W M Davis, Harriet	
Pendleton,	1901 Feb 16 Pendleton, J H	W F Law, Elizabeth M	
Perkins, Eugene Melville	1905 Mar 13 Perkins, Fred J	W M Lovelace, Maud	
Permort,	1894 Oct 15 Permort, Charles Laidort	W M Carr, Beryl	
Permort,	1899 Nov 16 Permort, Charles	W F Carr, Beryl	
Permort, Eunice Beryl	1897 Mar 25 Permort, Chas	W F Carr, Beryl	
Perry,	1900 Apr 25 Perry, Charles	W M Smith, Mable	
Peterson,	1900 Jan 17 Peterson, John	W F Anderson, Anna	
Peterson,	1901 Oct 12 Peterson, Emil	W M Kvisvik, Gaerlerie	
Peterson,	1902 Feb 13 Peterson, Chris	W M Christianson, Sophia	
Peterson,	1905 Apr 24 Peterson, R W	W M Dalton, _____	
Peterson,	1905 June 18 Peterson, John	W M Sungrun, _____	
Peterson,	1905 Oct 22 Peterson, Otto	W M Lindberg, Anna	
Peterson, Myrtle Malvina	1904 July 14 Peterson, Phillip	W F Stanbaugh, Myrtle	
Petrie,	1906 Jan 19 Petrie, John	W M Loach, Mary	
Pettibone,	1902 Jan 31 Pettibone, Walter	W M Latrobe, Dotty	

Boulder, Colorado Births, 1892-1906

Pettijohn, Gelena	1898 Apr 22 Pettijohn, Granville	W F Porter, Sadie
Pettit, Ella May	1893 Sept 17 Pettit, Samuel G	W F Melke, Elizabeth Jane
Phillips,	1895 June 20 Phillips, John S	W M Ott, Agnes
Pickel,	1893 Feb 2 Pickel, Robert	W M Shappard, Hester
Pickel,	1902 Mar 19 Pickel, Robert	W M Shapard, Hattie
Pickett,	1902 Mar 22 Pickett, Harry	W F Hastrom, Amanda
Platt,	1905 Nov 26 Platt, Milo E	W M Davis, Bertha E
Pode,	1902 Nov 11 Pode, Louis F	W M Bangel, Lulu H
Poole, Mary Ellen	1903 July 13 Poole, Wm Edward	W F Sullivan, Mary
Portman,	1905 Dec 20 Portman, Jno D	W M Hayes, _____
Potter,	1902 Aug 29 Potter, Wm	W M Martin, Marie
Potter,	1906 Jan 4 Potter, E L	W F Smith, _____
Potter, Ralph	1903 Apr 29 Potter, William	W M Whitsitt, Lena
Pouder,	1899 July 6 Pouder, Howard	W M Baker, Nellie
Powell,	1906 Jan 29 Powell, Luther I	W M Lovitts, Lulu
Powell, Alice	1899 Dec 20 Powell, Ralph Ralston	W F Lytle, Edyth Luella
Powers,	1906 June 23 Powers, Ira Elihue	W F Coxey, Katherine
Pratt,	1905 May 18 Pratt, Jefferson	W F Kirby, Myrtle

Boulder, Colorado Births, 1892-1906

Price,	1896 July 22 Price, Benjamin	W F Stewart, Libbie
Pritchard,	1895 Nov 14 Pritchard, D N	W F Heffeman, Lorena
Pugh,	1894 Jan 27 Pugh, Charles	W F Edwards, Ellen
Pughe,	1892 Sept 23 Pughe, John	W F Teal, Mary Ellen
Pughe,	1894 Nov 11 Pughe, John	W F Teal, Mary Ellen
Pulliam, Robert	1901 June 29 Pulliam, Nathan	W M Rose, Frankie
Purdy,	1896 Oct 15 Purdy, George	W M Bridges, Ida
Raikes,	1905 May 23 Raikes, Geo	W F Hotchkiss, _____
Raikes, Harold	1903 Feb 9 Raikes, Geo	W M Hotchkiss, Jesse
Rainger,	1897 Nov 16 Rainger, William J	W F Eldred, Pearl L
Ramsden, Robert Reymial	1897 May 28 Ramsden, Percy Herbert	W M Benett, Maria
Ramsey, Glen	1904 Jan 20 Ramsey, Andrew H	W M Reed, Hattie
Ramsey, Grace	1904 Jan 20 Ramsey, Andrew H	W F Reed, Hattie
Randall, Ruth	1899 May 23 Randall, John M	W F McBride, Mary
Rasier,	1899 Nov2 Rasier, Charles	W F Rathbone, Lulu
Redding, Jas William	1906 Feb 3 Redding, E Floyd	W M Cowie, Isabelle
Reed,	1906 Jan 10 Reed, Chas H	W M Sampson, Jessie
Reed, Charlotte Baldwin	1895 Apr 18 Reed, Albert A	W F Howell, Lydia

Boulder, Colorado Births, 1892-1906

Reid, James Malcolm	1902 Apr 10 Reid, James M	W	M Applegate, Anna
Remington,	1894 Nov 29 Remington, Walter Wood	W	M Porter, Sarah
Reppy, (twins)	1905 Nov 29 Reppy, James Henry	W	M Soderland, Mabel E
Reynolds,	1906 Feb 7 Reynolds, Christie E	W	M Blackwell, _____
Richard,	1896 Jan 5 Richard, Harry	W	M Heath, Nancy
Richards,	1900 Oct 14 Richards, Harry	W	F Harvey, Jennie
Riddle, Josephine	1902 May 15 Riddle, G D	W	F Tittle, Lizzie
Riley,	1900 Apr 13 Riley, W R	W	M Snyder, Ida
Robbins,	1904 Aug 24 Robbins, H O	W	F Morgan, _____
Roberts,	1896 Nov 20 Roberts, John	W	M Lewis, Hattie
Roberts,	1899 May 2 Roberts, A F	W	M Conger, Elmira J M
Robeson,	1894 May __ Robeson, William C	W	F Wannemaker, Nellie R
Roles,	1905 Oct 2 Roles, Medan	W	F Stalle, _____
Rose, Doris	1903 July 14 Rose, Albertus W	W	F House, Hattie
Rosen,	1904 Jan 10 Rosen, Oscar F	W	F Peterson, Jennie
Rosen, Oscar	1905 Dec 17 Rosen, Oscar F	W	M Peterson, Jennie
Ross,	1893 Dec 22 Ross, C N	W	F Johnson, Hannah
Ross,	1902 June 19 Ross, James A	W	M Hulliher, Minnie

Boulder, Colorado Births, 1892-1906

Rouse,	1892 July 14 Rouse, A E	W M Euler, Carrie	
Rowe,	1898 Apr 22 Rowe, Geo H	W M Whitmore, Grace	
Rowland,	1893 Dec 24 Rowland, Charles W	W M Van Dusen, Alice	
Rowland, Bessie	1896 Jan 24 Rowland, C W	W F Van Dusen, Alice	
Rowland, Dorris DeEtte	1900 Oct 11 Rowland, H E	W F Parker, Hattie	
Rowland, Joe Giffin	1898 Mar 11 Rowland, Charles W	W M Van Dusen, Alice	
Rudeen, Clarence	1902 Jan 1 Rudeen, Fred M	W M Sundgren, Olive	
Rumbel, Edna Pearl	1903 Oct 20 Rumbel, Jno N	W F Bottoms, Josie	
Runell, Mary Elora	1903 Feb 22 Runell, Charles	W F Horn, Elizabeth	
Russell,	1894 Sept 20 Russell, Charles A	W F Phelps, M Jennie	
Russell, Daniel S	1902 Sept 9 Russell, M E	W M Snyder, A C	
Russell, James Earl	1986 July 22 Russell, James Earl	W M Fletcher, M A	
Rutherford,	1904 June 10 Rutherford, Calvin	W F Ferree, Nannie R	
Sackett,	1892 July 30 Sackett, James N	W M Jones, Maud	
Sahn,	1900 Feb 18 Sahn, Henry	W M Hugg, Adina	
Sale, George Alfred	1893 Jan 29 Sale, George Pierce	W M Cole, Mary Alvira	
Salisbury, Ludia Irene	1898 July 15 Salisbury, L B	W F West, Lydia	
Salsbury, Melford Hawley	1903 Dec 21 Salsbury, John	W M Hawley, Martha	

Boulder, Colorado Births, 1892-1906

Sampson,	1900 Feb 26 Sampson, Horace Osborne	W F Smith, Jennie L	
Sanguinette,	1898 Dec 9 Sanguinette, Peter L	W F Conders, Louisa	
Sanguinette,	1900 Dec 27 Sanguinette, Peter L	W F Conders, Louisa	
Schuhman,	1903 Jan 16 Schuhman, David	W F Minks, Florence	
Scott, Wendell Garrison	1905 July 19 Scott, Ira D	W M Soper, Callie	
Seaburg,	1897 Feb 9 Seaburg, Chas	W M Hokensen, Emma	
Sears,	1895 May 27 Sears, Hiram A	W M Burton, Harriet A	
Sebring, Bonnie Beatrice	1902 Feb 26 Sebring, Frank E	W F Fanning, Emma A	
Seeburg,	1895 Sept 7 Seeburg, John	W F Hokensen, Emma	
Seeley,	1903 Aug 20 Seeley, Byron H	W F Clark, Louise	
Seeman, Louis Evert	1901 Aug 13 Seeman, Henry	W M Hutton, Mary	
Sellinghausen, Roy	1902 Mar 31 Sellinghausen, Louis	W M Abapfner, Mary	
Shall,	1894 June 6 Shall, Joseph	W F Bentley, Sarah	
Shall,	1897 Jan 6 Shall, Joseph	W F Bentley, Sarah	
Shane,	1896 Mar 4 Shane, E	W F Weiger, Ella	
Shankland,	1904 Sept 4 Shankland, William R	W F Richards, Celia	
Shapard, Maria	1903 June 15 Shapard, Robert L	W F Taber, Lillie B	
Shea,	1906 June 2 Shea, David	W M Cavanaugh, Bridey	

Boulder, Colorado Births, 1892-1906

Sheaffer,	1898 Aug 10	W	F
	Sheaffer, R A	Disbrow, Addie M	
Sherer,	1903 Dec 24	W	M
	Sherer, Joseph D	Brocker, Sophia Aleda	
Sherratt,	1898 Sept 3	W	M
	Sherratt, Frank	Whitaker, Irene A	
Sherwood,	1898 Sept 7	W	F
	Sherwood, Fred	Strickland, H L	
Shiber,	1903 Oct 21	W	M
	Shiber, J H	Ault, Myrtle	
Shinkle, Marie Viola	1897 June 14	W	F
	Shinkle, Wm S	Cook, Ada N	
Shreve,	1903 June 20	W	F
	Shreve, Geo E	Smith, Alice	
Shreve, Alice May	1902 May 2	W	F
	Shreve, G E	Smith, Alice I	
Shute,	1894 Mar 10	W	M
	Shute, Fred A	Carmack, Susie E	
Shutte,	1900 Jan 25	W	M
	Shutte,		
Siberts, Miriam	1905 Dec 1	W	F
	Siberts, Aubrey T	Lafferty, Myrtle U	
Sibley,	1892 Aug 6	W	M
	Sibley, Nat	Rouse, Gerdie	
Sidwell,	1902 May 10	W	M
	Sidwell, J E		
Sidwell, Mildred Eliza	1903 Dec 13	W	F
	Sidwell, Jerome E	Johnson, Martha	
Silcott,	1904 June 13	W	M
	Silcott, Perry	Nelson, Helen	
Simon,	1903 Aug 9	W	M
	Simon, Wm	Whitney, Cora	
Sisson,	1903 Jan 27	W	F
	Sisson, Charles	Hastings, Maud	
Smead, Effie Lavata	1892 Aug 23	W	F
	Smead, Charles C	Ripley, Hattie	

Boulder, Colorado Births, 1892-1906

Smith,	1898 Mar 6	W	F
	Smith, Minot	Clanton, Ada	
Smith,	1900 July 22	B	M
	Smith, R B	Davis, Lucinda	
Smith,	1901 Feb 7	W	M
	Smith, Leander	Clawson, Ethel	
Smith,	1903 Nov 10	B	F
	Smith, Chas M	McLeod, Mary E	
Snively,	1905 Jan 12	W	F
	Snively, Geo	Hershmon, Ella	
Snurtbar,	1894 Sept 30	W	F
	Snurtbar, Joseph	Woksa, Anna	
Sosey, Merl Theodore	1899 May 12	W	M
	Sosey, John	Hamm, Winnie	
Spier, *	1905 Sept 26	W	M
	Spier, Wm	Burlingame, Mary	
	* two certificates for this birth		
Spindler,	1896 Dec 3	W	M
	Spindler, F J		
Sprecher, Helen Margaret	1898 Mar 28	W	F
	Sprecher, Harry	Melwin, Mabel	
Squires,	1899 Aug 22	W	M
	Squires, A E	Thatcher, Samantha	
Stafford,	1892 Nov 11	W	M
	Stafford, Edward K	Kelly, Ida B	
Stafford, Sylvia Hyacinth	1902 Dec 24	W	F
	Stafford, E A	Cook, Dollie	
Staley,	1983 Jan 18	W	F
	Staley, Chas E	Davis, Mattie E	
Stanley,	1899 Sept 24	W	F
	Stanley, James	Hettenburg, Cora	
Stanton, Pearl	1899 Jan 27	W	F
	Stanton, Lewis H	Robinson, Ella L	
Starbuck,	1905 July 22	W	F
	Starbuck, Ira T	Logan, Grace	
Starkey,	1903 Mar 13	W	F
	Starkey, Clarence	Eby, Verna	

Boulder, Colorado Births, 1892-1906

Stary,	1900 Mar 22 Stary, Eugene	W F Long, Sarah
Stebenne,	1903 Sept 24 Stebenne, I C	W M Sexton, Mary
Stebenne,	1904 Dec 28 Stebenne, Isaac C	W F Sexton, Mary E
Stevens,	1898 Mar 30 Stevens, Henry	B M Venice, Louise
Stevens, Frank	1893 May 7 Stevens, Henry	B M Venice, Louise
Stevenson, Robert Llewellyn	1899 June 29 Stevenson, Harry H	W M Edwards, Mary E
Stewart,	1895 Mar 16 Stewart, W F	W M Green, Jennie
Stockton,	1905 Aug 19 Stockton, Charles	W F Ballinger, Ida B
Stockton, Alice Marie	1904 Nov 13 Stockton, Warren L	W F Nickum, ____
Stoggsdill, Alva	1895 Dec 30 Stogsdill, James	W M ____, Jenna
Stogsdill,	1897 July 26 Stogsdill, James	W M Stogsdill, Jennie
Stonehouse,	1899 Mar 21 Stonehouse, Jno W	W F Allen, Cora M
Stonhouse,	1896 Dec 14 Stonhouse, John W	W M Allen, Cora
Story,	1905 May 8 Story, W T	W F
Stragner,	1902 Jan 6 Stragner, R	W F Payton, ____
Strawhun,	1905 Oct 3 Strawhun, Thos M	W M Wardle, Sarah
Streamer,	1892 July 14 Streamer, F M	W M Walker, Lula
Sturdevant, Orpha	1902 Dec 17 Sturdevant, Thomas E	W F Linder, Hannah

Boulder, Colorado Births, 1892-1906

Sutter,	1904 Jan 31 Sutter, Laforest	W M Combs, Lilly
Svard,	1896 June 23 Svard, John	W M Larson, Anna
Sweet,	1902 Dec 11 Sweet, Alva H	W M Neptune, ____
Sweet,	1905 Jan 22 Sweet, Alva H	W F Neptune, May
Talley, Iva Norine	1896 July 12 Talley, Chas Isaac	W F Bernard, Laura A
Taylor,	1897 Oct 24 Taylor, Theodore	W M Large, Anna
Teal,	1903 Mar 8 Teal, George	W M Teal, Fannie
Temple,	1897 Aug 22 Temple, Harry	W M Lee, Rose
Teagarden,	1902 May 10 Teagarden, J A	W M Taylor, Olive
Terry, Harold	1898 Oct 20 Terry, Frank H	W M Lynch, Adeline
Thomas, Ernest Thomas	1904 Feb 28 Thomas, John Stewart	W M Smith, Norah
Thompson,	1892 June 21 Thompson, James A	W M Austin, Mattie
Thompson,	1896 Feb 23 Thompson, L E	W M Jeffers, ____
Thompson,	1896 Mar 17 Thompson, W H	W F Smith, Emma C
Thompson, Russell	1895 Sept 29 Thompson, Russ	W M Firstbrook, Laura
Tipps, Carl Logan	1903 July 30 Tipps, William A	W M Logan, Maud
Tipps, Helen	1901 Dec 15 Tipps, William	W F Logan, Maud
Tipps, Jessie Lucile	1899 Sept 22 Tipps, Wm A	W F Logan, Maud

Boulder, Colorado Births, 1892-1906

Tomlin,	1898 Sept 17	W	F
	Tomlin, John L	Ingram, Ida	
Tomlin, Kit	1902 Sept 18	W	F
	Tomlin, Marvin B	Alden, Lucy	
Tomlinson,	1898 Sept 6	W	M
	Tomlinson, A E	Handyshell, Lottie	
Town, Erma Margarette	1897 July 7	W	F
	Town, William	Ardourel, ___	
Towne,	1903 Jan 18	W	M
	Towne, Arthur J	Walk, Dora	
Townsend, Ethel	1895 May 3	B	F
	Townsend, Dick	Scruggs, Daisy	
Townsend, Ilene	1898 Apr 13	B	F
	Townsend, R W	Scruggs, Daisy	
Tracey,	1899 Sept 21	W	F
	Tracey, Geo E	Ball, Florence	
Tranger,	1906 July 14	W	F
	Tranger, Boyd	Carr, Lucy	
Tremelling,	1903 July 2	W	F
	Tremelling, Richard	Wasley, Minnie	
Truett, Archie R	1901 Jan 8	W	M
	Truett, G I	Cain, Ella	
Tucker,	1903 Apr 5	W	F
	Tucker, John	Roberts, Rosa	
Van Fleet,	1904 Apr 27	W	F
	Van Fleet, Edward	Munson, Augusta	
Van Fleet, Isabel Elnora	1902 July 15	W	F
	Van Fleet, E W	Munson, Augusta	
Vaplon,	1896 Mar 14	W	M
	Vaplon, William	Staples, Edith	
Vernon,	1899 Sept 29	W	M
	Vernon, Watson	Buckley, ___	
Vernon, Alva Alton	1904 July 1	W	M
	Vernon, Watson	Buckley, Loula	
Vinsonhaler, Vera	1903 July 17	W	F
	Vinsonhaler, Fred C	Haskins, Ethel E	

Boulder, Colorado Births, 1892-1906

Vivian,	1901 Dec 19 Vivian, John	W M Johns, Eunice
Waddy,	1898 Mar 17 Waddy, Ed	B M Simons, Alice
Wade,	1898 Nov 22 Wade, Harry	W M Santery, Adell
Wagner,	1892 June Wagner, Charles	W F Stevens, Anna
Walker,	1899 Aug 23 Walker, Henry H	W F Reed, Nellie L
Wallace,	1906 June 13 Wallace, Frank	W M Van Vranken, ____
Walsh,	1893 Jan 22 Walsh, J J	W F Powell, T A
Walsh,	1896 Oct 5 Walsh, Louis Eugene	W F Earl, Edna
Walsh,	1898 Feb 28 Walsh, Lou E	W M Hill, Edna
Walsh,	1899 June 16 Walsh, L E	W M Hill, Edna
Ward,	1895 Aug 24 Ward, Chas	W F Chevalier, Mary A
Ward,	1902 July 22 Ward, Charles B	W M Chevalier, Mary A
Ward, Ralph	1902 July 10 Ward, Frank	W M Adams, Frances
Warren,	1906 Jan 18 Warren, James Adolphus	W M Boyington, Bessie
Washburn, Flora Esther	1895 Oct 2 Washburn, Wm Burgett	W F Miller, Anna Maud
Waterman,	1895 Nov 7 Waterman, Fred	W M Breech, Esta
Waterman,	1896 Nov 20 Waterman, Fred	W F Breach, Esta
Watson,	1896 Apr 10 Watson, James	W M Scott, Carrie

Boulder, Colorado Births, 1892-1906

Watson,	1893 Sept 14 Watson, Vernon	W M Buckley, Lula	
Weber,	1897 Jan 18 Weber, Adam	W M Lytle, Alice	
Weber, Ethel Frances	1905 Mar 8 Weber, Adam	W F Lytle, Alice M	
Weber, Gretchen Alice	1901 Dec 1 Weber, Adam	W F Lytle, Alice M	
Weger,	1905 Oct 29 Weger, Fred	W M Shaw, _____	
Weist,	1900 Dec 19 Weist, John H	W F Malniovsky, Helen	
Weist, Elizabeth Catherine	1902 Oct 13 Wiest, John H	W F Malinowsky, Helen	
Wellman, Eugene Thesyl	1902 Sept 3 Wellman, Fred E	W M Boeshar, Emma	
Wells, Mina Austin	1902 Feb 25 Wells, Hugh L	W F Austin, Clara	
West, Frances	1905 Feb 13 West, Frank	W F Messinger, Edna F	
Whisler,	1899 Dec 18 Whisler, C A	W M Hamilton, Susan	
Whitaker,	1905 July 1 Whitaker, W E	W M Brendle, Marie C	
White,	1893 Aug 13 White, Fred	W M Ingram, Edith	
White,	1897 Feb 19 White, J C	W F Brierley, Emma A	
White,	1899 Sept 2 White, Fred	W M Ingram, Edith	
White,	1902 May 18 White, John C	W M Phillips, Mable	
White,	1903 June 4 White, Frederick	W F Ingram, Edith	
White,	1905 July 13 White, Fred	W F Ingram, _____	

Boulder, Colorado Births, 1892-1906

Whitney,	1895 Feb 18	W	F
	Whitney, Frank J	Porter, May	
Whitney, Gary Myron	1893 Feb 14	W	M
	Whitney, Edward Wilber	Taylor, Lizzie E	
Willen,	1898 July 24	W	F
	Willen, Asa	Rowland, Araminta	
Williams,	1903 Feb 14	W	M
	Williams, Maurice		
Williams,	1906 Feb 5	W	F
	Williams, Wm Morgan	Smith, Jane	
Williamson,	1894 Jan 21	W	F
	Williamson, Abram	Moffitt, Eliza A	
Williamson,	1898 Apr 25	W	M
	Williamson, Robert E	Bottoms, Alice	
Williamson,	1905 Oct 27	W	F
	Williamson, Robt E	Bottoms, _____	
Williamson, Robert Dudley	1893 Dec 28	W	M
	Williamson, Robert E	Bottoms, Dora Alice	
Willis,	1899 Mar 25	W	M
	Willis, Jas J	Ullmer, Mary E	
Wilson,	1903 Mar 23	B	F
	Wilson, Chas P	Brown, Ada M	
Wilson,	1903 Sept 11	W	F
	Wilson, Wm C	Hughes, Alice	
Wilson, Ina	1902 June 2	W	F
	Wilson, J M	Clough, Rillie	
Wilson, Ralph Eugene	1902 June 29	W	M
	Wilson, William	McGrew, Jessie	
Winder,	1905 Sept 7	W	F
	Winder, A H		
Wirick,	1900 Apr 5	W	M
	Wirick, Thomas	Fullwider, Ella	
Wirick, Paul C	1902 Oct 29	W	M
	Wirick, Thomas	Fullwider, Ella	
Wise,	1896 Aug 24	W	F
	Wise, Charles	Hamilton, Clara	

Boulder, Colorado Births, 1892-1906

Wolf,	1894 Sept 21　Wolf, W W	W M	Gibbon, Anna Jane
Wolff,	1905 June 21　Wolff, John R	W M	Hague, Maud
Wolverton, Merwin	1899 Aug 9　Wolverton, Edwin T	W M	Siprelle, W___ H
Wood,	1894 Mar 10　Wood, Albert S	W F	Hubbard, Minnie
Wood,	1896 Dec 18　Wood, Frank	W F	Adams, Philena
Wood, Leona	1904 Nov 26　Wood, Frank P	W F	Adams, Irine
Worrick,	1899 Jan 17　Worrick, Thomas	W F	Fulwider, Ella
Yates,	1895 Apr 3　Yates, Fred J	W F	Harris, Lizzie
Yates,	1905 Apr 28　Yates, Alva	W M	Munson, Hilda
Yockey,	1902 Sept 25　Yockey, Elmer	W F	Griffith, Elizabeth
Yockey,	1904 Apr 22　Yockey, Elmer	W M	Griffiths, ____
Younglove,	1903 Apr 18　Younglove, Charles B	W M	McLain, Mamie

Index

A

Abapfner
  Mary 49
Abbott
  Alta 24
  Alta L 24
Abernathy
  Martin L 5
Abrams
  Albert 5
  Dora Ellen 5
Adair
  Ada Belle Mary 5
  Andrew Adam 5
Adams
  Clara 30
  Clare 30
  Frances 55
  Guy Arthur 5
  Irine 58
  Jas B 5
  Philena 58
  Richard Thaddeus 5
Addams
  J H 5
  Pearl 5
Adler
  Rachel 5
  Solomen 5
Agee
  Kenneth 5
  Wm Grant 5
Akins
  Chas 5
  Mary W 24
Alden
  Lucy 54
Allaback
  J B 5
  John Bud 5
Allcorn 5
Allen
  Charles 5
  Cora 52
  Cora M 52
  Daisy M 30
  H W Jr 5
  Jennie 34
  Lillian 5
  Mildred 5
  O J 5
Allison
  Frank 5
Andersen
  Manda 9
Anderson
  Albertina 21
  Ana 19
  Anna 9, 44
  Emma 16, 28
  Emma Christine 28
  Florence 6
  Fred 5, 6
  Gussie 40
  Hilmer 6
  John 6
  John August 5
  Mary 30
  Mildred Adeline Gertrude 6
  Nora 33
Andre
  Albert 6
Andrews
  John 6
  Susie May 23
Angove
  Fred E 6
Anthony
  Mary R 15
Appeldorn
  Lou W 6
  Walter 6
Appledorn
  Walter 6
Applegate
  Anna 47

59

Boulder, Colorado Births, 1892-1906

Applegren
  Carl 6
  Effie Delilah 6
Archibald
  Chas H 6
  Robert Eldon 6
Ardourel 54
  Helen A 6
  Theopholus 6
Aronowitch
  Louis 6
  Mildred 6
  see Herman, L 26
Ary
  Minnie M 27
Ashcroft
  C B 6
Ashton
  David H 6
  William H 6
Attebury
  Ella 43
Atterberry
  Jennie 21
Atwood
  Joseph T 6
Ault
  Myrtle 50
Aumick 41
  May 25
Austin
  Clara 56
  Eugene A 6
  Mathie 26
  Mattie 53
Autrey
  Roy Sterling 6
  Thomas 6
Axelson
  G A 7
Axford
  Ebenezer B 7

  Edwin 7
  Richard Samuel 7
Ayers
  Alma 11

B

Baber
  Sam 7
Bachelder
  Lula 7
  Wm A 7
Badgley
  Margaret 12
Bailey
  Dwight B 7
  Emma 38
  Joseph R 7
  Maggie E 30
Bair
  Joseph H 7
Baker
  Arthur 7
  Ema 43
  John W 7
  Nellie 45
  Peter 7
Balderson
  Katherine 38
Baldwin
  Inez B 41
  May 19
Ball
  Florence 54
Ballinger
  Ida B 52
Bangel
  Lulu H 45
Banglesdorf
  GeorgeEtta 9
Barbour
  L P 7
  Mary Malvina 7

Index

Barleau
  Elizabeth 5
Barlow
  Chas T 7
Barnes
  Evaline L 34
Barnett
  Marguerite Helen 7
  Wm 7
Barry
  Thomas E 7
Bartlett
  James 7, 8
  Reuel 8
Barton
  Fannie 27
Basanko 10
Battey
  Henry F 8
Battles
  Cluade Otis 8
  Geo W 8
  L Bert 8
Baum
  S W 8
Baundy
  Wm 8
Baylor
  Chas N 8
Bayse
  Guy 8
Beale
  Alta 5
Beall
  Elsie 38
Beals
  John P 8
Beard
  Herman Mills 8
  H W 8
Beary
  Margaret 13

Becker
  Clemence L 16
Beckwith
  Frank Louis 8
  Leonard 8
Beeson
  Isa 16
Begole
  Geo D 8
  Lydia Marie 8
Beidleman
  Henry 8
  Oscar 8
Bellman
  Ruth 8
  W S 8, 9
Belser
  Carl William 9
Benett
  Maria 46
Bennett
  A Janette 19
  Clayton 9
Benson
  Anna 5, 6
  Nelse 9
  Pete 9
  Thomas F 9
Bentley
  Sarah 49
Beole
  Nora 36
Bergstrom
  Jno 9
Berkley
  Benjamin 9
  Frank 9
  G M 9
  McKenzie 9
  Roland 9
Bernard
  Laura A 53

Boulder, Colorado Births, 1892-1906

Bernhauer
  Bessie 6
Bernsten
  Charles 9
Berron
  Minnie 5
Berry
  Harriet 7
Bertha 6
Beyer
  George 9
Billig
  James A 9
  William Clinton 9
Binns
  Bessie 26
  Frankie 8
Binz
  Bessie 26
Birkett
  Mary 6
Bixby
  Jesse A 9
  Wallace Edgar 9
Black
  David 9
  Ralph 9
Blackburn
  Dorathen R 10
  Geo W 10
  Minerva 10
Blackwell 47
Blair
  Mary 36
Blixt
  Tholdo 9
Block
  Jennie 29
Blomquist
  Emelia 43
Blosser
  Jacob 10

  Ruby 10
  Ruth 10
Blum
  Conrad 10
  Virginia 10
Boche
  Charles W 10
Boecker
  Mary L 42
Boeshar
  Emma 56
Bohn
  Clara F 24
Boline
  Catherine 29
Bond
  Bertha 31
Bonelli
  Paul 10
Bonnel
  Leonora 10
Booth
  Ezra Horace 10
  Frank 10
  Walter L 10
  Walter Loyd 10
Borden
  Edmund J 10
  E J 10
Borlan
  Hattie 29
Bottoms
  Alice 57
  Catherine 37
  Dora Alice 57
  Josie 48
  Nannie J 8
  Walter Lee 10
Boulter
  John 10
  Phyllis 10
Boyd
  J W 10

Index

Boyer
　Carrie 16
Boyington
　Bessie 55
Boystatt
　Marie 29
Bracy
　Daniel H 10
　Doul C 11
　Ruby May 11
Bradfield 15
　Emma 18
Bradway
　Ruth 32
Brand
　Frank B 11
　Rudolph William 11
Brandon
　Jerry 11
Branford
　Alonzo 11
Breach
　Fred 11
Breech
　Esta 55
Brendle
　Marie C 56
Bridges
　Ida 46
Brierley
　Emma A 56
Brierly
　Cecil 11
　Sylvester 11
Brister
　Russell Laraine 11
　Wm R 11
Brocker
　Sophia Aleda 50
Brockway
　Alexander Grove 11
　Clara Mary 11

　W A 11
　William Ansley 11
Brohard
　Thomas Marion 11
Bromley
　Alice 42
　Charles C 11
　Charles Dunham 11
Bronson
　Elmer 11
　Henry 11
Brook
　Alberta C 5
Brooks
　E P 11
　Frank 11
　John W 11
Brown
　Ada M 57
　A H 11
　Charles A 12
　Charles Albert 12
　Chas C 12
　Dorothy 12
　Jno L 11, 12
　Leona 41
　Lizzie 5
　Margaret 12
　Newell Edward 12
　O N 12
　Sara 30
Brubaker
　H 12
Bruddenbock
　Marie 12
　William 12
Bruet
　Luvella M 35
Bryan
　Frank 12
　Ralph Arthur 12
Bryant
　J A 12

63

Boulder, Colorado Births, 1892-1906

Bucheit
  Emma 6
Buckingham
  Rosemary Greene 12
  Walter M 12
Buckley 54
  Loula 54
  Lula 56
Bueler
  Olive 33
Buffham
  Leslie 12
Bullard
  Otto W 12
Bumgarner
  Daisy N 22, 23
Burch
  Willis E 12
Burger
  Frances Marie 12
  Fred 12
  Fred W 12
Burgess
  Bruce 12
  Frankie 12
Burlingame
  Edna M 40
  Mary 51
Burton
  Harriet A 49
Bush
  Maud 34
Buslen
  Miles R 12
Butler
  Olive 32

C

Cacheman
  Margaret 41
Cain
  Ella 54
Calden
  Mike 12
Calkins
  Alman 13
  Almon K 13
Callahan
  Gilbert A 13
  Katherine G 13
Callender
  John L 13
Calton
  Sue 19
Cameron
  Maud 20
Campbell
  Birtha 37
  Lee 13
  Lida 23
Canall
  Harry 13
Cannon
  Myrtle E 25
Cantrall
  Carrie 10
Caper
  Horace 13
Carkener
  Geo S 13
Carlson
  John 13
Carlton
  Jane 36
Carmack
  John L 13
  Susie E 50
Carner
  Rose 32
Carpenter
  Elihu 13
  W H 13
Carr
  Beryl 44
  Edith 34

Index

Edna 10
Lois 28
Lucy 54
Carrie
  Alexander D 13
Carrothers
  Susie 6
Carsrud
  Gus 13
Casaday
  Arthur Lockwood 13
  Harry 13
Casey
  Catherine Julia 13
  J H 13
  John H 13
  Pat V 13
Cather
  Alma May 11
Catherwood
  Grace Adele 9
Cattell
  Bertha Luella 14
  Wm P S 14
Cattermole
  F P 14
  George 14
  G H 14
  Horace 14
Cavanaugh
  Bridey 49
Ceraton
  Virla 23
Chadbourne
  Martha 11
Chamberlain
  Pearl E 14
Chambers
  Mary 33
Chandler
  Walt 14
  Walter 14
  Charles P 16

Chase
  Harry Romeyn 14
  Julia 14
  Romeyn 14
Chasino
  Mary 30
Cherry
  Jessie F 8
Chesney
  Charles 14
  Gwendolyn Virginia 14
Chevalier
  Mary A 55
Cheyne
  Annie 31
Childers
  Thomas H 14
Ching
  Bertha 14
  Edward 14
  John Thomas 14
Choate
  Mortimer 14
Christianson
  Sophia 44
Churchill
  Edmund 14
Clanton
  Ada 51
Clark
  Carrie 39
  E A 14
  Ellsworth A 14
  Elvira Virginia 42
  H M 14
  J A 15
  Jesse E 15
  Louise 49
  Roy R 14
Clawson
  Ethel 51
Cline
  Robert W 15

Boulder, Colorado Births, 1892-1906

Clough
   Rillie 57
Coates
   Edwin L 15
   Edwin Wilder 15
Cobb
   Chas F 15
Coffman
   Mitchell Hughes 15
Colborn
   Geraldine Hope 15
   Jno A 15
Cole
   Belle F 17
   Mary Alvira 48
Collins
   Angela 15
   Mary A 7
   William P 15
   W P 15
Collinson
   Selma 26
Combs
   Lilly 53
   Robt 15
Conders
   Louisa 49
Conger
   Elmira J M 47
Connor
   Esther 42
Cook
   Ada N 50
   Dollie 51
Coons
   H R 15
Corbett
   Howard 15
   Pierce 15
Corey
   Etta 19
Coring
   Frieda 13

Cork
   Josephine 31
Cornell
   Clara 20
Corning
   Frieda 13
Coslett
   James 15
   Ruth 15
Costen
   Edith E 7
Coulehan
   Charles E 15
Coulson
   Harry 15
Cowan
   Elsie F 38
Cowie
   Isabelle 46
Coxey
   Katherine 45
Craig
   C H 16
   Clarence H 15
   Harry Becker 16
   Jennie 31
Crandall
   Don 24
Crary
   J H 16
   John Howard 16
Crawford
   Roy G M 16
Crimmins
   Bert 16
Critchfield
   Joe 16
Crockett
   Katharine Thomas 16
   Thomas W 16
Cronin
   Elizabeth 35

Index

Crosby
  Herbert 16
  Jennie 38
  Roscoe 16
Crosman
  Everett S 16
Crouch
  Frank 16
  John E 16
  Stanton N 16
Culbertson
  Charles 16
  Edward Alexander 16
Cummings 17
Curran
  John 16
Curtis
  Electa May 16
  Frank Edward 16
  Geo C 16

D

Dalton 14, 44
  Ella 25
  Isaac N 17
  Joseph 16
  Julia 36
  Lenore 17
  Martin 16
  Susie 17
Daugherty
  Frank 17
Davidson
  Adeline 40
Davis
  Abram A 17
  Agnes 41
  Bertha E 45
  Emma 41
  Gertrude 15
  Harriet 44
  Kathleen Helen 17
  Lucinda 51
  Mary 36
  Mary E 41
  Mary M 37
  Mattie E 51
  Mina 15
  Nellie 14
  Sidney C 17
Dawson
  Benj M 17
  Florence 17
Day
  Helen 17
  John W 17
  Timothy F M 17
DeBacker
  Frank 17
Decker
  Henry Snyder 17
DeGroot
  Rachel 19
  Ray 19
Demmon
  Wm R 17
Denham
  A L 17
  Alonso 17
  Alonso L 17
DePriz
  Eugene 17
Derby
  Fred 17
Derr
  Joe 17
  Joe E 17
  Sarah 7
  William 17
DeRusha
  Elijah 17
Deutch
  P J 18
DeVoss
  J Wm 18

Boulder, Colorado Births, 1892-1906

DeWalt
  Robert 18
Dickensheets
  Larson 18
Dickson
  Dennis H 18
Disbrow
  Addie M 50
Dittemore
  Helen Alene 18
  James 18
  James H 18
Dollar
  Mamie 26
Donaghue
  Terrance 18
Donaldson
  A R 18
  John Andrew 18
Dora J 8
Dovina
  Rose 30
Downs
  Martha 16
  Rose 37
Dragoo 18
  Julius M 18
Drumm
  Alta Catherine 18
  John B 18
Drummond
  Alvie 18
Duane
  William 18
Dubi
  J J 18
Duncan
  E E 19
  J M 19
  John 19
  Myrtle M 19
  R A 19
  Robert A 18, 19

Dungan
  F R 19
Dunham
  Edward Bennett 19
  Elbert L 19
  Helen Frances 19
  Maurice E 19
  Theresa 11
Dunn
  Herbert 19
  Joe 19
Durfee
  Henry C 19
  Henry Gordon 19
Dutcher
  Minnie 42
Dutton
  Flavilla 12

E

Earl
  Edna 55
Eastland
  Anna 20
Eastman
  Elmer O 19
Eaton
  Frank A 19
  Robert 19
Eatsman
  Elmer 19
Eby
  Verna 51
Eddy
  Jessie 18
  Jessie A 18
Edelhoff
  E 19
Edwards
  Annie 23
  Bertie 35
  Ellen 46
  Mary E 52

Index

Eggler 34
Eggleston
  Louisa 15
  Louisa A 15
Ehrlich
  Frieda 19
  Louis 19
  Louis U 19
  Marcella 19
Eislinger
  Lillie P 27
Eldred
  Pearl L 46
Elkins
  Belra 19
  Jesse R 19
Ellison
  A E 20
Emanual
  Alma 35
Engert
  Daisy 34
Epperly
  Dewey 20
  Howard 20
Erickson
  Arthur 20
  Lewis 20
Ericson
  Lenni 22
Eskdahl
  Alma 6
Esslinger
  Lillie 28
Etteford
  Ida 16
Etz
  Emma 31
Eubank
  Maude 35
Euler
  Carrie 48
  Edward 20
  Emma 20
  Isabelle 12
  R L 20
  Wm Jr 20
Evan
  Edith 37
Evans
  Nell 13
  Sadie 34
Ewing
  Frederick G 20
  Howard Ellert 20

F

Fabrizio
  Peter A 20
Fagerstedt 38
Faivre
  Anna 12
  Louise 29
Fanning
  Emma A 49
Farley
  Mabel 40
Faurot
  L Alice 20
  William Augustus 20
Ferguson
  Nettie 22
Ferree
  Nannie R 48
Fields
  Sanford 20
Figlia
  A 20
  Dominick 20
Filion
  Arthur 20
Fink
  Emma 36
Firstbrook
  Laura 53
  Thomas 20

Boulder, Colorado Births, 1892-1906

Firth 43
Fisher
  Julia 20
  William P 20
  William Peter 20
Flannery
  Lena 42
Fletcher
  M A 48
Flickenger
  Maggie 19
Foher
  Lionel 21
Fondi
  Josephine 36
Foote
  Adelaide 26
Forbes
  Delia 25
Forbus
  Ella 15
Fordis
  Sarah 28
Foreman
  Elsie 13
  Mabel 24
Forsythe
  E E 21
  Elijah E 21
  Tamer 35
Fox
  J Y 21
Frankfathers
  Josephine E 28
Fraser
  Geo W 21
Frekes
  W H 21
Freman
  Elsie 29
Friday
  F J 21

Friel
  Amelia 6
Friend
  Bernice Ethel 21
  Chas 21
Fritter
  Ruth 28
Fry
  Adelaide M 10
  Chas 21
  William Clyde 21
Fuller
  Grace 29
Fullwider
  Ella 57
Fulwider
  Ella 57, 58

G

Galattie
  Angus 21
Galusha
  Benjamin F 21
  Mary 28
  Wm 21
Gamble
  Elizabeth Louise 21
  Harry P 21
Garborino
  Lida 39
Gardner
  Anna 13
  Arthur C 21
  F J 21
  Wm Hartley 21
Gates
  Clara 21
  Eugene E 21
Gause
  Elmer O 21
Gee
  Mattie E 21

Index

George
  W S 22
Gerhart
  Charles 22
Gerison
  George A 22
Geromunger
  Maud Etta 22
  William P 22
Gibbon
  Anna Jane 58
Giffin
  Grace Lake 22
  Horace L 22
  L M 22
Giggey
  Charles 22
  Clair Leon Morris 22
  Laura 34
  Lydia 24
Giggy
  Leon 22
  Myrtle 27
Gilbert
  Carrie 23
  Carson W 22
  Chas T 22
  Eduard 22
  Irene 10
  Isabel Maurine 22
  Mildred Jane 22
  O M 23
  Oscar M 22
  Rachel 23
Gilbrand
  Charles T 23
Gill 11
Gillard
  W W 23
Giller
  Albert 23
  Charles Robert 23

  Janet 23
  Thos E 23
Gilmore
  Jno T 23
Girandet
  Frederick 23
Glazier
  Jas W 23
Goddard
  Clint Morton 23
  Edith E 17
  Frank M 23
Goodro
  Joseph 23
Goodwin
  Walter 23
Gordan
  Cora L 12
Gordeono
  Glen 23
Gore
  Eugene Herald 23
  R M 23
Goslen
  Emma 33
Gothe
  Mary Ellsworth 23
  Victor E 23
Gould
  Margaret Rache 23
  Roy 23
Graham
  Chas J 23
  Margaret 23
  Robert E 24
  Robert Elisha 24
  Wm 23
Graves
  Edgar Raymond 24
  Grace 15
  John G 24
Green
  Charles Arthur 24

Boulder, Colorado Births, 1892-1906

Jennie 52
June Louise 21
Maude 15
William Henry 24
Greene
  Cora 24
  Janil B 12
Gregg
  Frank 24
  George Coabran 24
  Mabel 9
  Orlando G 24
  Orlando W 24
Greisheim
  R C 24
Greshaber
  J C 24
  Joseph C 24
Griffith
  Elizabeth 58
Griffiths 58
Gross
  Abner T 24
  C C 24
  George William 24
Grove
  Sarah Sophia 11
  S S 11
Gruier
  John G 24
Grusbury
  Cora 39
Gumeson 41
  John 24
Gunneson
  Chas 24
  Marguerite 24
Gustafson
  Charlotte 26

H

Hagman
  Charlotte Marie 24

  Chas 24
  Melvin Andrew 25
Hague
  Maud 58
Haight
  Grace 27
Hain
  Wm 25
Haitt
  Ruphema 16
Hales
  C A 25
Hall 6
  Charles 25
  Dewey 25
  Elizabeth M 25
  G A 25
  Harriett 42
  Welcome 25
  William Earl 25
  Wm H 25
Hallett
  George 25
  W H 25
Halps
  Georgiana C 38
Ham
  William H 25
Hamilton
  Clara 57
  Clara Louise 43
  Susan 56
Hamm
  Winnie 51
Handyshell
  Lottie 54
Hankens
  C E 25
  Ray Estef 25
Hankins
  Della 28
  Lula 37

Index

Hanks
  William W 25
Hansen
  Minnie 24
Hanson
  Andrew C 25
Hardin
  Clara S 31
Hardy
  Irving 25
Harlow
  Howatson 25
  William Page 25
Haroley
  LeRoy 25
Harris
  Claire M 19
  Della 34
  Emma 38
  Lizzie 58
  Margarett 31
  Walter 26
  Walter Stewart 26
  William 25
Harrison
  Benj F 26
Hart
  Bert 17
Harvey
  Jennie 47
  Louise 15, 16
Haskey
  Georgia 29
Haskins
  Ethel E 54
Haslip
  William 26
Hastings
  Maud 50
Hastrom
  Amanda 45
Hatfield
  Sidney A 26

Haugh
  Henry 26
Haviland
  David A 26
  David J 26
  Jean Delphine 26
Hawkins
  Elton E 26
  Prince A 26
  Ziemer 26
Hawley
  Martha 48
Hayes 45
  W B 26
Hays
  Frank A 26
Healy
  Alva I 26
Heath
  Nancy 47
Heck
  Myral 29
Hecker
  Elizabeth 34
Hector
  Adolph A 26
  George 26
Hedeman
  Frederika Matilda 26
  John F 26
Hedlund
  Hayes 26
Heffeman
  Lorena 46
Heivener
  Doris 22
Heller
  Della 30
Helps
  Georgina 38
Hendon
  Erastus T 26

Boulder, Colorado Births, 1892-1906

Hendter
  Elizabeth 42
Henry
  May 10
Herkert
  Fred 26
Herman
  (formerly Aronowitch) 26
  L 26
Hershmon
  Ella 51
Hettenburg
  Cora 51
Hetzel
  Sam J 27
  Samuel D 27
Hewitt
  O E W 27
Hickman
  Emmett 27
  Helen Louise 27
Hicks
  Joseph E 27
Higgins
  Mary 33
Hill
  Alya 30
  E B 27
  Edna 55
  Edward L 27
  Edward T 27
  Elizabeth 7
  E T 27
  Frank W 27
  George Barney 27
  Matilda 27
  Ruth Blair 27
Hillberry
  Ella M 40
Hilton
  C W 27
Hilts
  Samuel 27

Hinkle 33
  J P 27
Hinman
  Curt 27
Hipple 26
Hite
  Cedella 40
Hixson
  Carthryn White 27
  Howard 27
Hockaday
  Edmund W 27
Hocking
  Elmer V 27
  E U 28
  Wm W 27
Hoffman
  Cliff 28
Hoke
  Mary 37
Hokensen
  Emma 49
Holborn
  Mary 8
Holland
  R O 28
Hollingsworth
  Anna 26
Holly
  Josie 30
Holman
  Thos B 28
Holstein
  Beatrice Ruth 28
  Harry C 28
Holt
  Ora 35
Hoover
  William Rex 28
  Wm L 28
Hopper
  Thos P 28

Index

Horn
  Elizabeth 48
Horry
  Grant Garfield 28
  James 28
Hotchkiss 46
  Jesse 46
House
  Hattie 47
  Melissa Jane 31
Howard
  Cora 38
  Minora 17
Howatson
  Jean 25
Howe
  Albert E 28
Howell
  Lydia 46
  Millie 12
  Walker 28
Hoyer
  August L 28
  Carl Walfred 28
Hoyle
  Camie 42
Hubbard
  Charles 28
  Minnie 58
  William H 28
  William James 28
Hubbel
  Theron E 28
Hubman
  Chas 28
  Karl 28
Hudson
  Maggie 28
Hugeltno
  Alice Lucretia 28
  John 28
Hugg
  Adina 48

Hughes
  Alice 57
Hull
  Ella 37
  Grant 28
Hulliher
  Minnie 47
Hunt
  Linfield Harold 28
  Linfield V 28
Hunter
  Ella H 11
  Sarah L 10
Hupp
  twins 29
  Wm 29
Hurtencin
  Alma 40
Huschleffe
  J N 29
Hussey
  Maud M 11
Hutchinson
  Charlotte 16
Hutton
  Mary 49

I

Imel
  Alonzo C C 29
Infield
  J H 29
Ingalls
  Harry D 29
  Harvey Munson 29
Ingals
  M 29
Ingram
  Edith 56
  Edwin 29
  E J 29
  Ida 54

Boulder, Colorado Births, 1892-1906

Isard
  Alva 29
  Frances 29
  Izora 17

J

Jabas
  Genevieve 14
Jacka
  Marion M 29
  Thos 29
Jackson
  Amanda 26
  F H 29
Jacobson
  Nils 29
Jain
  Ben 29
  B F 29
  Clyde 29
  Zerleta 29
James
  Alex 29
  Alfred 30
Jay
  Rosa 29
Jeffers 53
Jenna 52
Jenner
  Delbert Oren 30
  William 30
Jennie B 29
Jermo
  Andrew 30
  Beatrice 30
Jester
  Loretta 34
Johns
  Eunice 55
Johnson
  Alvah 30
  Amanda 24
  Amos 30
  Augusta 9
  Bettie 33
  Cora 25
  Frank 30
  Hannah 47
  Jennie 35
  Martha 50
  Minnie 9
  Niti B 9
  Peter C 30
  Wesley 30
  Wm A 30
Johnston
  Frank 30
  Lawrence Allen 30
  Louis R 30
  William J 30
  Wm J 30
Jones 30
  Daniel Thomas 30
  Dorr Theophilus 30
  Earl R 30
  Frank 30
  Mark 30
  Maud 48
Joratz
  Frankie M 20
  Joe 30
Jordinelli
  Frank 30
  John 30
Joss
  Willie 31
  Wm 31
Joyce
  Bernard 31
  William Edward 31
Jump 33
Junior
  Adolph 31

Index

K

Kaler
  Charles F 31
  Fred H 31
Karns
  John P 31
Kealiher
  Clarence 31
Keen
  Estella L 32
Kelley
  Hattie 20
Kellogg
  M M 31
  Nellie 38
Kelly
  Gerdie L 42
  Ida B 51
Kemmler
  Ernest 31
Kempton
  Mabel 41
Kendrick
  Sam 31
Kenyon
  Della 36
Kern
  Estella 32
Kerr
  C E 31
Kestle
  Preston 31
  Thomas 31
Killier
  David 31
  Thurllyn 31
King
  J N 31
  Wm F 31
Kingman
  Annie 31
  Henry 31

Kinsman 29
  F J 31
Kirby
  Myrtle 45
Kirkbride
  Agnes 22
  Annie 8, 9
Kittle
  Harl S 31
  Josephine Blanche 31
Klee
  Maggie T 13
Klinger
  Clara 12
Knapp
  Geo 32
Knaus
  Tillie 25
Knight
  George 32
  Harry 32
  Harry Stewart 32
Knopf
  E J 32
Knott
  Sam'l G 32
Knowlton
  Carroll F 32
  George Theodore 32
Knox
  Chester 32
  Randolph B 32
Kohler
  Charles S 32
  Fred Jr 32
Kramer
  Frederick Ferdinand 32
  Frederick Sprague 32
  John Spalding 32
Kuhepass
  Geo A 32
Kvisvik
  Gaerlerie 44

Boulder, Colorado Births, 1892-1906

L

Labbo
  Frank 32
Lacer
  Chas 32
Lachepelle
  Ida 17
Lafferty
  Myrtle U 50
Lake
  Fannie M 22
  H C 32
  Mary Marguerite 33
Lakin
  Frank 33
Lamb
  M T 33
  Ogden Frances 33
Lambert
  Fred 33
Lamm
  Alice 33
  Wm 33
Large
  Anna 53
Larsen 24
  C R 33
Larson
  Albert 33
  Anna 53
  Emma 12, 30
  Jennie 42
  Matilda 26
  Mildred 33
  Peter A 33
  William John 33
Latora
  Felix 33
Latrobe
  Dotty 44
Laughlin
  Mable 23

Laurence
  Albert 33
Lauretzen
  Katy 41
Law
  Elizabeth M 44
Lawrence
  Cora 14
  D E 33
  Henry 33
Lawson
  William S 33
Lee
  Annie 31
  John H 33
  Rose 53
Leech
  Dorothy 33
  William F 33
Leland
  Lyman W 34
Lemmex
  Frank 34
  Iola Elizabeth 34
Lennertz
  Herman 34
Levinton
  James 34
  twins 34
Levy
  Rebecca 28
Lewis
  E C 34
  E C Jr 34
  Edward 34
  Grant 34
  Harry 34
  Hattie 47
  Helen 34
  Kenneth Carr 34
  Nat 34
  Nathaniel 34
  Nathaniel Fancy 34

Index

O A 34
W C 34
Libby
  Eleanor Clare 34
  M F 34
Liethe
  Minnie 20
Lilly
  John E 34
Lincoln
  Stanton 34
Lindberg
  Anna 44
Linder
  Chris 34
  Hannah 52
Lindermann
  Ernest 34
  Reece 34
Lindley
  Georgia L 20
Lindstrom
  Chas 35
Lines
  G W 35
Lingham
  Abraham 35
  Frank 35
Litch
  H F 35
  Rodney Marion 35
Little
  Maggie 18
Littlejohn
  Elizabeth 36
Lizzie 17
Loach
  Mary 44
  William 35
  William Jennings 35
Logan
  Grace 51
  Maud 53

Long
  Charles W 35
  Leon 35
  Sarah 52
Longhi
  Albert W 35
Loofboro
  Chase A 35
Lorpee
  Georgia 41
Louth
  James 35
Love
  Cora M 14
  Cora May 14
Lovelace
  Maud 44
Lovitts
  Lulu 45
Low
  Clara Ellen 30
Lowe
  J M 35
Lowrey
  Charles Emmet 35
  Mary 35
Ludlow
  Julia 40
Luman
  Bertha 24
Lunburg
  Gustove E 35
Lundrie
  Peter P 35
Lundstrom
  Hulda 22
Lurman
  Mary 21
Lurvid
  Charles 35
Lynch
  Adeline 53

Boulder, Colorado Births, 1892-1906

Lynor
  Elizabeth 35
  John M 35
Lyon
  Edgar 35
Lytle
  Alice 56
  Alice M 56
  Edyth Luella 45

M

Mace
  Myra M 11
Machens
  Ada 8
  Ada P 8
Mackey
  Richard 36
Magee
  Catherine 36
  John 36
Main 21
Malinowsky
  Helen 56
Malniovsky
  Helen 56
Mamie 10
Man
  Bertha 18
Mansen
  N Campbell 43
Marian
  John 36
Marino
  Joseph 36
Markley
  Sadie 11
Marr
  Wm Nolan 36
Marriott
  Fred 36
Marro
  Antonio 36

Marshall
  Neata Agnes 36
  R T 36
Martin
  John 36
  Julia 10
  Marie 45
  Samuel 36
  Wm R 36
Mason
  Barbara 36
  E C 36
  Geo W 36
  Isabel 36
  J D 36
Mathews 41
  Frank 36
  Kate 21
  Lida 31
Matters
  Thos 36
Maud 21
Maxwell
  Ada 43
  Alice A 12
  Charles Alonzo 36
  Della 36
Mayad
  Ada Louise 36
  Harry 36, 37
  Samuel Tully 37
Mayall
  Harry 37
  Henry Hale 37
  May Lucy 37
  Sarah J 37
McAllester
  Daniel E 37
  Marion E 37
McAllish
  Daniel Eldridge 37
  Marjorie Mansfield 37

Index

McAllister
  Ethel 27
McBride
  Mary 46
McCall
  Francis 32
  George 37
  George Willard 37
McCammon
  Annie 22
McCare
  John 37
McCarl
  Elsworth 37
McCaslin
  Adeline 6
McClora
  A 37
McClure
  George A 37
McColly
  James F 37
McConnell
  Nettie 15
  Porter 37
McDonald
  Jas 37
  Sarah Isabelle 37
McDowell
  Andrew S 37
McFadden
  Lou S 37
  Lura D 28
McFarland
  Mary 17
McGady
  Catherine 40
McGee
  Sadie 5
McGinnis
  Wm 37
McGrew
  Jessie 57

McIntosh
  Jennie 29
McIntyre 8
McKelvey
  Roy E 38
McKenna
  Harry 38
McLain
  Mamie 58
McLean
  Christine 37
McLeod
  Mary E 51
McLilton
  Eugene E 38
McLinnis
  John 38
McMasters
  Barbara 38
  P H 38
McMillan
  F H 38
McVey
  J 38
  J D 38
  J W 38
Mecham
  Edward U 38
  Paul Willis 38
Meeker
  Edna 12
  Estelle 20
Meginnes
  Harold 38
  W H 38
Meikle
  Agnes 38
  Archibald 38
  Geo 38
Meisele
  Johanna 39
Melke
  Elizabeth Jane 45

Boulder, Colorado Births, 1892-1906

Mellor
  James Herbert 38
  Margaret Elizabeth 38
Melwin
  Mabel 51
Mendenhall
  Elisha F 38
Meredith
  J Q 38
  Leland 38
Merrill
  E T 39
  Myrtle Zoella 39
Merrow
  Leona 8
Messenger
  Claudius L 39
  Elmer 39
Messinger
  Edna F 56
Metcalf
  Frank P 39
  Geo E 39
  Laura Lee 39
  Lewis M 39
  L M 39
Metz
  Dena 12
Meyer
  Max 39
Meyring
  Nettie 22
Michelson
  John W 39
Middleton
  Theron Cecil 39
  Wm W 39
  W W 39
Mila
  Josie 36
Miles
  Leslie P 39
  Lizzie 37

Milker
  H H 39
Miller 37
  Anna Maud 55
  Arnold 39
  G E 39
  Hattie 39
  J O 39
  John O 39
  LeRoy H 39
Milligan
  Fannie O 34
Millin
  Ivy Myrtle 21
Milne
  Robert 39
Milner
  Harvey E 40
Minks
  Florence 49
  May 6
  Minnie F 42
Mischler
  Susan 9
Mishle
  Clare 7
Mitchel
  Fred 40
  Lizzie 32
  Sidie 13
Mitchell
  Chase 40
  Fred 40
  John Charles 40
Mock
  Isaac 40
  Will T 40
Moeller
  Peter 40
Moffitt
  Eliza A 57
Money
  Kenneth 40

Index

Monroe
  D N 40
  Margerate 13
Montgomery
  B L 40
  Hattie 30
  Jack Reemier 40
  Nellie 40
  Walter A 40
Moon
  Anna Lucylle 40
  John D 40
  Williw O 40
Moore
  Catherine Gertrude 40
  Mary L 39
  William Y 40
Morgan 47
  Catherine L 18
Morrell
  Anthony 40
  Irene Frances 40
Morrison 39
  M S 40
Morro
  Antonio 40
Morton
  Elsie R 26
Moseley
  C B 41
  Geo B 41
Mosely
  Chas B 41
  Luekan Garber 41
Moses
  Nora 23
Mosher 8
Muchenhaupt
  Gail 25
Mudd
  Don A 41
  Don Alexis 41

Munson
  A L 41
  Anna 6
  Augusta 54
  Hilda 58
  William LeRoy 41
Murphy
  G H 41
Murray
  Izelle 5
Mushblond
  Edgar 41
Musley
  Annie 23
Myers
  Jas M 41
  Martha 23

N

Neiheisel
  Dorothy Grace 41
  Wm 41
Neikirk
  Fannie 6
Nelmer
  Charles 41
Nelms
  Hubert 41
Nelson
  Adam W 42
  Alexander 41
  Anna 41
  Arvi 41
  Ernest 41
  Ethel 41
  Harriet 27
  Helen 50
  James 41
  Lois Marie 42
  L R 41
  Mamie 22
  N P 41
  P B 41

83

Boulder, Colorado Births, 1892-1906

Petrus 41
Selma 41
Neptune 53
  May 53
  Nettie 22
Neufert
  Chadwick 42
Neville
  Chesley W 42
Newberry
  Fannie 28
Newcomb
  Clarence W 42
  Laura Leola 42
Newell
  Mabel 25
Newhouse
  Harry R 42
Nichols
  Walter H 42
  Webb W 42
Nicholson
  J H 42
Nickum 52
Niederber
  Frank 42
Nielson
  Anna 25
Ninsie
  Artie 30
Noel
  Ethel 39
Nordquist
  Nels 42
Norlin
  Agnes Marguerette 42
  George 42
Norman
  R C 42

O

O'Connor
  Clarence J 42
  Daniel 42
  Jno 42
  Jno Robert 42
  Robert Clark 42
Oden 42
Oest
  Mary 8
Ogden
  Anna 33
  Eugene 42
Ohelder
  Hattie 14
Oliver
  John N 43
  Will J 42
Orr
  Anna Ellen 13
  Annie E R 13
Ory
  Minnie 27
  Winnie M 27
Osborn
  Chas 43
Otis
  Hampton J 43
Ott
  Agnes 45
Owen
  Lucrete B 43
  William C 43
Owens
  Mary M 23

P

Pack
  Minnie 24
Paddock
  Frank Smith 43
  Kenneth Larden 43
Page
  Andrew F 43
  Frank K 43

Index

Harry J 43
Ralph Attebury 43
Palmer
  Chas P 43
  Dorothy Hamilton 43
  Frederic Armine 43
  Henry H 43
  Millie 21
  Winifred W 43
Parcells
  Arthur 43
  E W 43
Parker
  Hattie 48
  Mattie 18
Parks
  Alvin Thomas 43
  Geo B 43
  Ida 25
  Ida L 25
  Reuel Lois 43
Parsons
  J A 43
  Joseph 43
  Joseph H 43
  Margaret Eliza 43
  Mattie 6
  William James 43
Pate
  Edgar 43
  Ethel Pearl 43
Patterson
  Orlando 43
Patton
  A C 44
  Mada 44
Payne
  Hattie 13
Payton 52
Pease
  Gertrude 14

Peasley
  LeRoy 44
  LeRoy Verner 44
Pendleton
  J H 44
Perkins
  Eugene Melville 44
  Fred J 44
Permort
  Charles Laidort 44
  Eunice Beryl 44
Perry
  Charles 44
Peters
  Pauline 33
Petersen
  Inya M 41
Peterson
  Chris 44
  Emil 44
  Jennie 47
  John 44
  Minnie 43
  Myrtle Malvina 44
  Otto 44
  Phillip 44
  R W 44
Petrie
  John 44
Pettibone
  Walter 44
Pettijohn
  Gelena 45
  Granville 45
Pettit
  Ella May 45
  Samuel G 45
Phelps
  M Jennie 48
  Sarah S 6
Phillips
  Agnes 34
  Anna 31

Boulder, Colorado Births, 1892-1906

Belle 22
Emily 43
John S 45
Mable 56
Philpy
　Olive G 13
Pickel 45
　Lulu 10
　Robert 45
Pickett
　Harry 45
Pierce
　Lilly 15
Pinkham
　Abigail 36
Platt
　Milo E 45
Pode
　Louis F 45
Pomeroy
　Leah 23
Poole
　Mary Ellen 45
　Wm Edward 45
Porter
　May 57
　Sadie 45
　Sarah 47
Portman
　Jno D 45
Potter
　E L 45
　Genevieve 24
　Ralph 45
　William 45
　Wm 45
Pouder
　Howard 45
Powell
　Alice 45
　Luther I 45
　Ralph Ralston 45
　T A 55

Powers
　Ira Elihue 45
Pratt
　Jefferson 45
Price
　Benjamin 46
　Ellen 28
Primey
　Ella 27
Pritchard
　D N 46
Pugh
　Charles 46
Pughe
　John 46
Pulliam
　Nathan 46
　Robert 46
Purdy
　George 46

Q

Quinn
　Lillie 27

R

Rachofsky
　Dora 39
Raikes
　Geo 46
　Grace W 33
　Harold 46
Rainger
　William J 46
Ramsden
　Percy Herbert 46
　Robert Reymial 46
Ramsey
　Andrew H 46
　Glen 46
　Grace 46

Index

Randall
  John M 46
  Ruth 46
Randolph 19
  Bertha 11
  Geraldine 43
Raplon
  Anna 21
Rappa
  Maggie 32
Rasier
  Charles 46
Rathbone
  Lulu 46
Ravenal
  Caroline Elsie 18
Raybourne
  Florence 7
Reardon
  Hannah 26
  Mary 23
Redding
  E Floyd 46
  Jas William 46
Reed
  Albert A 46
  Charlotte Baldwin 46
  Chas H 46
  Hattie 46
  Mary L 16
  Nellie L 55
Reedy
  Martha A 12
Reid
  James M 47
  James Malcolm 47
  Nellie 39
Remington
  Walter Wood 47
Reppy
  James Henry 47
  twins 47

Retallack
  Louise 43
Reynolds
  Christie E 47
Rhinesheimer
  Marian 5
Richard
  Harry 47
Richards
  Celia 49
  Harry 47
  Jennie 36
Richardson
  Blanch 5
  Lilly 21
  Mary 16
Riddle
  G D 47
  Josephine 47
Rider
  Cora 35
Riley
  W R 47
Ripley
  Hattie 50
Robbins
  H O 47
Roberts
  A F 47
  John 47
  Rosa 54
Robertson
  Elizabeth 13
Robeson
  William C 47
Robinson
  Annie S 32
  Ella L 51
Rockwell
  Mamie 34
Rockwood
  Emma 35

Boulder, Colorado Births, 1892-1906

Rodgers
　Jennie F 16
Roles
　Medan 47
Rose
　Albertus W 47
　Doris 47
　Frankie 46
　Gertrude 21
Rosen
　Oscar 47
　Oscar F 47
Ross
　C N 47
　Eunty 39
　Florence 18
　James A 47
Rouse
　A E 48
　Gerdie 50
Rowe
　Geo H 48
Rowland
　Araminta 57
　Bessie 48
　Charles W 48
　C W 48
　Dorris DeEtte 48
　H E 48
　Joe Giffin 48
　Lucy Ellen 8
Rudeen
　Clarence 48
　Fred M 48
Rumbel
　Edna Pearl 48
　Jno N 48
Runell
　Charles 48
　Mary Elora 48
Russell
　Charles A 48
　Daniel S 48
　James Earl 48
　M E 48
Rutherford
　Calvin 48

S

Sabin
　Anna M 21
Sachett
　Carrie E 21
Sackett
　James N 48
Saggan
　Minnie 7
Sahn
　Henry 48
Sailor
　Alma 14
Sale
　George Alfred 48
　George Pierce 48
Salisbury
　L B 48
　Ludia Irene 48
Salsbury
　John 48
　Melford Hawley 48
Sambaugh
　Ana M 19
Sampson
　Horace Osborn 49
　Jessie 46
Sanguinette
　Peter L 49
Santery
　Adell 55
Sauer
　Maude 7
Sawyer
　Amy E 13
Sayler
　Elinor 14

Index

Schneider
　Mollie 16
Schuhman
　David 49
Scofield
　Mary 25
Scott
　Annett 20
　Carrie 55
　Ira D 49
　Wendell Garrison 49
Scruggs
　Daisy 54
　Lulu 35
Seaburg
　Chas 49
Sears
　Hiram A 49
Sebring
　Bonnie Beatrice 49
　Frank E 49
Seeburg
　John 49
Seeley
　Byron H 49
Seeman
　Henry 49
　Louis Evert 49
Selcott
　Alice 41
Sellers
　Mattie M 33
Sellinghausen
　Louis 49
　Roy 49
Sexton
　Mary 52
　Mary E 52
Shall
　Joseph 49
Shane
　E 49

Shankland
　William R 49
Shannon
　Bertha 27
Shapard
　Hattie 45
　Maria 49
　Robert L 49
Shapherd
　Blanche 11
Shappard
　Hester 45
Sharon
　Annie 5
Shaw 56
　Mary 12
Shea
　David 49
Sheaffer
　R A 50
Shear
　Minnie 11
Sheppard
　Ida 33
　Sadie 15
Sherer
　Annie 18
　Joseph D 50
Sherman
　Anna 16
　Maude 17
Sherratt
　Frank 50
Sherwood
　Fred 50
Shiber
　J H 50
Shinkle
　Marie Viola 50
　Wm S 50
Shope
　Rose 21

89

Boulder, Colorado Births, 1892-1906

Short
  A Lyda 17
  Sarah 38
Shreve
  Alice May 50
  G E 50
  Geo E 50
Shumway
  Maud E 25
Shute
  Fred A 50
  Pearl A 40
Shutte 50
Siberts
  Aubrey T 50
  Miriam 50
Sibley
  Nat 50
Sida
  Mary 31
Sidwell
  Emma 6
  J E 50
  Jerome E 50
  Mildred Eliza 50
Silcott
  Perry 50
Simon
  Wm 50
Simons
  Alice 55
Siprelle
  W 58
Sisson
  Charles 50
Slater
  Jessie 9
Slattery
  Mary 36
Sly
  Bessie 40

Smead
  Charles C 50
  Effie Lavata 50
Smith 45
  Ada 33
  Alice 50
  Alice I 50
  Bertie 43
  Chas M 51
  C J 27
  Emma C 53
  Jane 57
  Jeanette 17
  Jeanette Orr 17
  Jennie L 49
  Leander 51
  Mabel 8
  Mable 44
  Minot 51
  Nevada 31
  Norah 53
  R B 51
  Susan A 7
Snively
  Geo 51
Snook
  Nellie 29
Snurtbar
  Joseph 51
Snyder
  A C 48
  Ida 47
  Katie 28
Soderland
  Mabel E 47
Soper
  Callie 49
Sorley
  Anna 32
Sosey
  John 51
  Merl Theodore 51

Index

Spaulding
  Lena 16
Spicer
  Etta 7
  Julia 43
Spieler
  Melinda 19
Spier
  Wm 51
Spindler
  F J 51
Sprague
  Ada Josephine 32
Sprecher
  Harry 51
  Helen Margaret 51
Springsteel 19
  Dora 20
  Stella 19
Spurre
  Hannah 13
Squires
  A E 51
Stafford
  E A 51
  Edward K 51
  Sylvia Hyacinth 51
Staley
  Chas E 51
Stalle 47
Stallings
  Ora 26
Stanbaugh
  Myrtle 44
Stanley
  Ida 16
  James 51
Stansberry
  Flora M 5
Stanton
  Lewis H 51
  Pearl 51

Staples
  Edith 54
Starbuck
  Ira T 51
Starkey
  Clarence 51
Stary
  Eugene 52
Stebenne
  I C 52
  Isaac C 52
Stephens
  Elsie 32
Stephenson
  Marie 14
Stevens
  Anna 55
  Belle 38
  Frank 52
  Henry 52
Stevenson
  Harry H 52
  Ida 6
  Mary 8
  Robert Llewellyn 52
Stewart
  Libbie 46
  Mary 10
  W F 52
Stockton
  Alice Marie 52
  Charles 52
  Warren L 52
Stoggsdill
  Alva 52
Stogsdill
  James 52
  Jennie 52
Stonehouse
  Jno W 52
Stonhouse
  John W 52

91

Boulder, Colorado Births, 1892-1906

Storey
  Ida 31
Story
  W T 52
Stragner
  R 52
Strawhun
  Thos M 52
Streamer
  F M 52
Strickland
  H L 50
Strottemire
  Lula May 43
Struble
  Grace 20
  Grace May 20
Sturdevant
  Orpha 52
  Thomas E 52
Sullivan
  Mary 45
Sundgren
  Olive 48
Sungrun 44
Sutter
  Laforest 53
Sutton
  Lillian 14
Svard
  John 53
Sweet
  Alva H 53
  Nellie 30
Sykes
  Georgiana E 28

T

Taber
  Lillie B 49
Talley
  Charles Isaac 53
  Iva Norine 53
Tanner
  Jane 27
Taylor 31
  Lizzie E 57
  Olive 53
  Sarah Annie 5
  Theodore 53
Teagarden
  J A 53
Teal
  Fannie 53
  George 53
  Mary Ellen 46
Temple
  Harry 53
Teormu
  Maggie 9
Terry
  Frank H 53
  Harold 53
  LaNicsa 20
Thatcher
  Samantha 51
Thayer
  Myrtle 36
Thiel
  Edith 15
Thomas
  Ernest Thomas 53
  John Stewart 53
Thompson 11
  Carrie E 12, 40
  James A 53
  L E 53
  Mary Glover 35
  Russ 53
  Russel 53
  W H 53
Tipps
  Carl Logan 53
  Helen 53
  Jessie Lucile 53
  Wiliam A 53

Index

William 53
Wm A 53
Tittle
  Lizzie 47
Titus
  Effie M 6
  Luella B 13
Todd
  Violet H 35
Tomlin
  John L 54
  Kit 54
  Marvin B 54
Tomlinson
  A E 54
Town
  Erma Margarette 54
  William 54
Towne
  Arthur J 54
Towner 13
Townsend
  Dick 54
  Ethel 54
  Ilene 54
  Margaret 40
Tracey
  Geo E 54
Tracy
  Adelina 42
Tranger
  Boyd 54
Treadwell
  Stella 12
Tremelling
  Richard 54
Trevarton
  Edith 18
Truett
  Archie R 54
  G I 54
Tucker
  John 54

Tulley
  May 36
Tully
  May 37
Tydeman
  Carrie 42
Tyler
  Bessie L 41

U

Ullmer
  Mary E 57
Urie
  Jula 23
Urst
  Mary 11

V

Vance
  Mary 36
Van Dusen
  Alice 48
Van Fleet
  Edward 54
  E W 54
  Isabel Elnora 54
Van Vranken 55
Vaplon
  William 54
Venice
  Louise 52
Vernon
  Alva Alton 54
  Essie 32
  Watson 54
Veslick
  Hattie 42
Vinsonhaler
  Fred C 54
  Vera 54
Vivian
  John 55

Boulder, Colorado Births, 1892-1906

Vogt
  Christina 17

W

Waddy
  Ed 55
Wade
  Arm 41
  Arminta 38
  Harry 55
Wagner
  Charles 55
Walk
  Dora 54
Walker
  Helen Jane 30
  Henry H 55
  Lula 52
Wallace
  Frank 55
  Mae 33
Walsh
  J J 55
  L E 55
  Lou E 55
  Louis Eugene 55
Wannemaker
  Nellie R 47
Ward
  Charles B 55
  Chas 55
  Frank 55
  Ralph 55
Wardenburg
  Lulu 27
Wardle
  Sarah 52
Warner
  Essie 14
  Essie M 14
  Harriet 43
  Minnie 16

Warren
  James Adolphus 55
Washburn
  Flora Esther 55
  Wm Burgett 55
Wasley 17
  Minnie 54
Waterman
  Fred 55
Watson
  James 55
  Vernon 56
Watts
  Isabelle F 21
Weber
  Adam 56
  Ethel Frances 56
  Gretchen Alice 56
Wedlake
  Louisa Jane 24
Weger
  Fred 56
Weiger
  Ella 49
Weist
  Elizabeth Catherine 56
  John H 56
Wellman
  Belle 29
  Clara B 29
  Eugene Thesyl 56
  Fred E 56
Wells
  Hugh L 56
  Leta 26
  Leta B 26
  Mina Austin 56
West
  Frances 56
  Frank 56
  Lydia 48
Whisler
  C A 56

Index

Whitaker
  Irene A 50
  W E 56
White
  Daisy 41
  Ella 37
  Emma 35
  Fred 56
  Frederick 56
  J C 56
  John C 56
  Minnie Ada 39
  Nanie 11
  Susie H 20
  Vallie P 27
Whitmore
  Grace 48
Whitney
  Cora 50
  Edward Wilber 57
  Frank J 57
  Gary Myron 57
Whitsell
  Maud 39
Whitsett
  S Maud 39
Whitsitt
  Lena 45
Whyte
  Ruth Margaret 34
Wilcox
  Ora 23
Wilder
  Florence 15
Willen
  Asa 57
Williams
  Emma A 40
  Mabel 33
  Maggie 38
  Maude D 5
  Maurice 57
  Wm Morgan 57

Williamson
  Abram 57
  Robert Dudley 57
  Robert E 57
Willis
  Anna 11
  Jas J 57
Wilson
  Chas P 57
  Ida 15
  Ina 57
  J M 57
  Lena 9
  Ralph Eugene 57
  William 57
  Wm C 57
Winder
  A H 57
Winters
  Katie 16
Wirick
  Lulu 7, 8
  Paul C 57
  Thomas 57
Wise 14
  Charles 57
Woksa
  Anna 51
Wolf
  Harriet E 25
  W W 58
Wolfesberger
  Louisa 18
Wolff
  John R 58
Wolverton
  Edwin T 58
  Merwin 58
Wood
  Albert S 58
  Frank 58
  Frank P 58
  Leona 58

95

Boulder, Colorado Births, 1892-1906

Ruth 31
Woods
  Millie 5
  Minnie 24, 31
Worrick
  Thomas 58
Wright
  Cena 19
  Myrtle M 19
  Myrtle May 18, 19
  Nellie 34
Wyatt 28

Y

Yates
  Alva 58
  Fred J 58

Yerkey
  Carrie 39
Yockey
  Elmer 58
Young
  Mary 7
Youngblood
  Marion J 18
Younglove
  Charles B 58

Z

Ziemer
  Myrtle 26

www.ingramcontent.com/pod-product-compliance
Lightning Source LLC
Chambersburg PA
CBHW061457040426
42450CB00008B/1396